Irvine 08

TECHNOLOGIES OF THE SELF

Technologies

OF THE

Self

A SEMINAR WITH

MICHEL FOUCAULT

EDITED BY

LUTHER H. MARTIN

HUCK GUTMAN

PATRICK H. HUTTON

THE UNIVERSITY OF

MASSACHUSETTS PRESS

AMHERST

Copyright © 1988 by The University of Massachusetts Press

Printed in the United States of America

LC 87–10756

ISBN 0–87023–593–1 (paper)

Designed by Barbara Werden

Set in Linotron Janson at Rainsford Type

Printed by Cushing-Malloy and bound by John Dekker & Sons

Library of Congress Cataloging-in-Publication Data

Technologies of the self.

   1. Self (Philosophy) 2. Foucault, Michel—
Contributions in concept of the self. I. Foucault,
Michel. II. Martin, Luther H., 1937–   . III. Gutman,
Huck, 1943–   . IV. Hutton, Patrick H.
BD450.T39   1988   126   87–10756
ISBN 0–87023–593–1 (pbk. : alk. paper)

British Library Cataloguing in Publication data are available

CONTENTS

TECHNOLOGIES OF THE SELF

INTRODUCTION

Shortly before his death in 1984, Michel Foucault spoke of an idea for a new book on "technologies of the self." He described it as "composed of different papers about the self (for instance, a commentary on Plato's *Alcibiades* in which you find the first elaboration of the notion of *epimeleia heautou*, 'care of oneself'), about the role of reading and writing in constituting the self . . . and so on." [1] The book Foucault envisioned was based on a faculty seminar on "Technologies of the Self," originally presented at the University of Vermont in the fall of 1982. This volume is a partial record of that seminar.

Because Foucault died before he completed the revisions of his seminar presentations, this volume includes a careful transcription instead, together with a transcript of his public lecture to the university community on "The Political Technology of Individuals." Professor Foucault's seminar on "Technologies of the Self" at the University of Vermont stands as a provisional statement of his new line of inquiry. We offer this volume as a prolegomenon to that unfinished task.

In many ways, Foucault's project on the self was the logical conclusion to his historical inquiry over twenty-five years into insanity, deviancy, criminality, and sexuality. Throughout his works Foucault had concerned himself largely with the technologies of power and domination, whereby the self has been objectified through scientific inquiry (*The Order of Things*, 1966, trans. 1970) and through what he termed "dividing practices" (*Madness and Civilization*, 1961, trans. 1965; *The Birth of the Clinic*, 1963, trans. 1973; and *Discipline and Punish*, 1975, trans. 1977).[2] By 1981, he became increasingly interested in how "a human being turns him- or herself into a subject." [3]

Foucault had addressed the issue of the self already in volume 1 of *The History of Sexuality* (1976, trans. 1978), but there he was still concerned with the objectification of the self by the "increasing valorization of the discourse on sex." [4] He envisioned his new project, however, as "separate from the sex series." "I must confess," he reflected, "that I am much more interested in problems about techniques of the self and things like that rather than sex. . . . sex is boring." [5] His new project would be, rather, a genealogy of how the self constituted *itself* as subject.[6] In the Vermont seminar, he began an investigation of those practices whereby individuals, by their own means or with the help of others, acted on their own bodies, souls, thoughts, conduct, and way of being in order to transform themselves and attain a certain state of perfection or happiness, or to become a sage or immortal, and so on.[7]

In his final lecture to the University of Vermont community, Foucault summarized his concern with the self as an alternative to the traditional philosophical questions: What is the world? What is man? What is truth? What is knowledge? How can we know something? And so on. In the tradition of Fichte, Hegel, Nietzsche, Weber, Husserl, Heidegger, and the *Frankfurterschule*, Foucault was interested in the question he understood to have appeared at the end of the eighteenth century with Kant: "What are we in our actuality?" "What are we today?"—that is, "the field of the historical reflection on ourselves." [8]

According to Foucault, his project on the self was suggested by a reading of Christopher Lasch's *The Culture of Narcissism* (1978). Foucault understood Lasch's description of disillusionment with the modern world and a subsequent turning within to be similar to the situation of the Roman Empire. Breaking with his starting point of the classical age, the pivotal period in his previous analyses until *The History of Sexuality*, Foucault located the roots of the modern concept of the self in first- and second-century Greco-Roman philosophy and in fourth- and fifth-century Christian spirituality, two different contexts that he understood to be in historical continuity.

Foucault's six seminar presentations trace the techniques of self-formation from the early Greeks to the Christian age. They gain their focus from an examination of classical texts, which Foucault expounded from their original languages. As with much of Foucault's work, the importance of these inquiries lies not only in their contribution to the specific history of the period but to what he called the history of the present—an excavation of and perspective on the bedrock of our modern conceptions.

Foucault had insisted that the work of the seminar be collaborative. His ideas on the historical constitution of the self, though extraordinarily clear, were not fully developed, and he valued the discussion—even the opposition—that his ideas engendered. This volume includes, therefore, selected revised presentations by members of the seminar. They represent historical investigations on the common theme of the seminar.

In contrast to the technologies of the self explored in the seminar by Foucault from the Western ethical tradition, Luther Martin looks at the Eastern techniques of self, which entered the Western tradition only with the influence of the monk John Cassian. He discovers a concern with "taking care of oneself" that is as central to the Syrian Thomas tradition, an early form of Gnostic Christianity, as to the West, but as an interdiction rather than an obligation.

William Paden compares the techniques of self-scrutiny prescribed by Cassian and those set out by the New England Puritans. He finds that they represent two radically different ways of dealing with subjectivity: On the one hand is the monk's confident renunciation of self followed by a life of purity, and on the other hand is the Puritan's implicit acceptance of selfhood but with attendant suspicions about its deceptive character.

Kenneth Rothwell, too, is interested in religious technologies.

Locating *Hamlet* at that historical moment when the Reformation emerged, he sees in Hamlet's radical transformation the personification of a change in the technologies of self which is consonant with the replacement of earlier religious practices by the new practices of the Reformation.

Huck Gutman examines Rousseau's *Confessions* in order to delineate a newly emergent Romantic sense of self. He focuses on various techniques— confession, division, flight to the ideal—which are used by Rousseau for fashioning this new self and making it visible. Gutman concludes by showing that these technologies are finally insufficient for Rousseau's purposes and that they lead him not to the constitution but to the negation of the self.

At the conclusion of the seminar, it seemed important to compare Foucault's method with that of Sigmund Freud, whose psychoanalytic technique has provided the basis of most of this century's theorizing about the nature of the psyche. Patrick Hutton's essay shows how Foucault's look at the ancient lineage of methods for care of the self provides a counterpoint to Freud's quest to discover the self's true nature. Foucault's genealogical investigation of past technologies of the self not only provides an original perspective on Freud's work but also reveals a sustaining line of continuity in his own scholarly endeavor over twenty-five years.

NO ENDEAVOR of this sort can come to fruition without the work and support of many people. President Lattie F. Coor of the University of Vermont originated and provided the funds for the Vermont Seminars, which sponsored the seminar. Dr. Robert Stanfield, Assistant to the President, helped us through countless difficulties in bringing the idea to reality.

Rux Martin, a free-lance writer, made the written transcript of Foucault's seminar. She also contributed her interview with

Foucault in which he discusses some of the influences—both emotional and intellectual—upon his thought.

Several scholars came to the university to comment on Foucault's work: Frank Lentricchia, Professor of Literature at Duke University, author of *After the New Criticism*; Christopher Lasch, Professor of History at the University of Rochester, author of *The Culture of Narcissism*; and Allan Megill, Professor of History at the University of Iowa, author of *Prophets of Extremity: Nietzsche, Heidegger, Foucault, Derrida*.

Most importantly, we would like to thank the university faculty who helped plan and participated in the seminar and who guaranteed its success. Participants committed a good deal of their time to this project. They read and met regularly to discuss all of Foucault's work in preparation for his coming. During the three weeks that Foucault was on campus, they met twice weekly with the seminar in addition to attending public events, which included lectures by Lasch, Megill, and Foucault and a showing of the film *I, Pierre Rivière . . .*, followed by a wide-ranging discussion led by Foucault. This project was an unusually intensive and productive venture by colleagues working on a common theme.

Michael Foucault's boldness and rigorous honesty in the quest for knowledge are well known. His presence, however, was not what might be expected from reading his works. Those who had expected a stern and distant scholar were surprised by his gentle humor. A sought-after lecturer, he was nonetheless shy and had to be urged to take the stage during public presentations. He shunned what he called "intellectual cocktail parties," but he was interested in nearly everything: in the life of the university as well as academic subjects, in the politics of Burlington, in the local night life. He was interested in the views of children and at the homes of faculty members would spend much of the evening talking with them about their concerns. He was happiest in the company of students, whom he sought out in classes, in the library, in the cafeteria. Those who met him noticed most of all

8

his eyes: penetrating, inquisitive, joyous. We remember him for his vitality, his generosity, his belief in the validity of all experience.

This volume is dedicated to his memory.

Notes

1   Paul Rabinow and Hubert L. Dreyfus, "How We Behave: Interview with Michel Foucault," *Vanity Fair*, November 1983; p. 62.

2   Michel Foucault, "The Subject and Power," Afterword to Hubert L. Dreyfus and Paul Rabinow, *Michel Foucault: Beyond Structuralism and Hermeneutics* (Chicago: University of Chicago Press, 1982), p. 208.

3   Public lecture to a conference on "Knowledge, Power, History: The Humanities as a Means and Object of Criticism," sponsored by the Center for the Humanities, University of Southern California, October 1981; published as the first part of Foucault's Afterword, in Dreyfus and Rabinow, *Foucault*, pp 208–9.

4   Michel Foucault, *The History of Sexuality, vol. 1: An Introduction*, trans. Robert Hurley (New York: Pantheon, 1978), p. 23; see also p. 70.

5   "How We Behave," p. 62.

6   See *The History of Sexuality*, vol. 2: *The Use of Pleasure*, trans. Robert Hurley (New York: Pantheon 1985), p. 11, where Foucault reconceived his original project on sexuality as part of a "general history of the 'techniques of the self.' "

7   See Foucault, "Technologies of the Self," herein. For some of these themes, but still in the context of his work on sexuality, see *The History of Sexuality*, vol. 3: *The Care of the Self*, trans. Robert Hurley (New York: Pantheon, 1986), pp. 37–68.

8   Immanuel Kant, "Was heisst Aufklärung?" *Berliner Monatschrift*, 1784. See Foucault, Afterword, in Dreyfus and Rabinow, *Foucault*, p. 214.

One TRUTH, POWER, SELF:

AN INTERVIEW WITH MICHEL FOUCAULT

OCTOBER 25, 1982

RUX MARTIN

Q: Why did you decide to come to the University of Vermont?

A: I came to try to explain more precisely to some people what kind of work I am doing, to know what kind of work they are doing, and to establish some permanent relationships. I am not a writer, a philosopher, a great figure of intellectual life: I am a teacher. There is a social phenomenon that troubles me a great deal: Since the 1960s, some teachers are becoming public men with the same obligations. I don't want to be a prophet and say, "Please sit down, what I have to say is very important." I have come to discuss our common work.

Q: You are most frequently termed "philosopher" but also "historian," "structuralist," and "Marxist." The title of your chair at the Collège de France is "Professor of the History of Systems of Thought." What does this mean?

A: I don't feel that it is necessary to know exactly what I am. The main interest in life and work is to become someone else that you were not in the beginning. If you knew when you began a book what you would say at the end, do you think that you would have the courage to write it? What is true for writing and for a love relationship is true also for life. The game is worthwhile insofar as we don't know what will be the end.

My field is the history of thought. Man is a thinking being. The way he thinks is related to society, politics, economics, and history and is also related to very general and universal categories and formal structures. But thought is something other than societal relations. The way people really think is not adequately analyzed by the universal categories of logic. Between social history and formal analyses of thought there is a path, a lane— maybe very narrow—which is the path of the historian of thought.

Q: In *The History of Sexuality*, you refer to the person who "upsets established laws and somehow anticipates the coming freedom." Do you see your own work somewhat in this light?

A: No. For a rather long period, people have asked me to tell them what will happen and to give them a program for the future. We know very well that, even with the best intentions, those programs become a tool, an instrument of oppression. Rousseau, a lover of freedom, was used in the French Revolution to build up a model of social oppression. Marx would be horrified by Stalinism and Leninism. My role—and that is too emphatic a word—is to show people that they are much freer than they feel, that people accept as truth, as evidence, some themes which have been built up at a certain moment during history, and that this so-called evidence can be criticized and destroyed. To change something in the minds of people—that's the role of an intellectual.

Q: In your writing you seem fascinated by figures who exist on the margins of society: madmen, lepers, criminals, deviants, hermaphrodites, murderers, obscure thinkers. Why?

A: I am sometimes reproached for selecting marginal thinkers instead of taking examples from the mainstream of history. My answer will be snobbish: It's impossible to see figures like Bopp and Ricardo as obscure.

Q: But what about your interest in social outcasts?

A: I deal with obscure figures and processes for two reasons: The political and social processes by which the Western European societies were put in order are not very apparent, have been forgotten, or have become habitual. They are a part of our most familiar landscape, and we don't perceive them anymore. But most of them once scandalized people. It is one of my targets to show people that a lot of things that are a part of their landscape—that people think are universal—are the result of some very precise historical changes. All my analyses are against the idea of universal necessities in human existence. They show the arbitrariness of institutions and show which space of freedom we can still enjoy and how many changes can still be made.

Q: Your writings carry profound emotional undercurrents unusual in scholarly analyses: anguish in *Discipline and Punish*, scorn and hope in *The Order of Things*, outrage and sadness in *Madness and Civilization*.

A: Each of my works is a part of my own biography. For one or another reason I had the occasion to feel and live those things. To take a simple example, I used to work in a psychiatric hospital in the 1950s. After having studied philosophy, I wanted to see what madness was: I had been mad enough to study reason; I was reasonable enough to study madness. I was free to move from the patients to the attendants, for I had no precise role. It was the time of the blooming of neurosurgery, the beginning of psychopharmacology, the reign of the traditional institution. At first I accepted things as necessary, but then after three months (I am slow-minded!), I asked, "What is the necessity of these things?" After three years I left the job and went to Sweden in great personal discomfort and started to write a history of these practices [*Madness and Civilization*].

Madness and Civilization was intended to be a first volume. I like to write first volumes, and I hate to write second ones. It was perceived as a psychiatricide, but it was a description from history. You know the difference between a real science and a

pseudoscience? A real science recognizes and accepts its own
history without feeling attacked. When you tell a psychiatrist his
mental institution came from the lazar house, he becomes
infuriated.

Q: What about the genesis of *Discipline and Punish?*

A: I must confess I have had no direct links with prisons or
prisoners, though I did work as a psychologist in a French prison.
When I was in Tunisia, I saw people jailed for political
expediency, and that influenced me.

Q: The classical age is pivotal in all your writings. Do you feel
nostalgia for the clarity of that age or for the "visibility" of the
Renaissance when everything was unified and displayed?

A: All of this beauty of old times is an effect of and not a reason
for nostalgia. I know very well that it is our own invention. But
it's quite good to have this kind of nostalgia, just as it's good to
have a good relationship with your own childhood if you have
children. It's a good thing to have nostalgia toward some periods
on the condition that it's a way to have a thoughtful and positive
relation to your own present. But if nostalgia is a reason to be
aggressive and uncomprehending toward the present, it has to be
excluded.

Q: What do you read for pleasure?

A: The books which produce in me the most emotion: Faulkner,
Thomas Mann, Malcolm Lowry's *Under the Volcano.*

Q: What were the intellectual influences upon your thought?

A: I was surprised when two of my friends in Berkeley wrote
something about me and said that Heidegger was influential
[Hubert L. Dreyfus and Paul Rabinow, *Michel Foucault: Beyond
Structuralism and Hermeneutics* (Chicago; University of Chicago
press, 1982)]. Of course it was quite true, but no one in France
has ever perceived it. When I was a student in the 1950s, I read
Husserl, Sartre, Merleau-Ponty. When you feel an overwhelming

influence, you try to open a window. Paradoxically enough, Heidegger is not very difficult for a Frenchman to understand: When every word is an enigma, you are in a not-too-bad position to understand Heidegger. *Being and Time* is difficult, but the more recent works are clearer.

Nietzsche was a revelation to me. I felt that there was someone quite different from what I had been taught. I read him with a great passion and broke with my life, left my job in the asylum, left France: I had the feeling I had been trapped. Through Nietzsche, I had become a stranger to all that. I'm still not quite integrated within French social and intellectual life. As soon as I can, I leave France. If I were younger, I would have immigrated to the United States.

Q: Why?

A: I see possibilities. You don't have a homogenous intellectual and cultural life. As a foreigner, I don't have to be integrated. There is no pressure upon me. There are a lot of great universities, all with very different interests. But of course I might have been fired out of them in the most outrageous way.

Q: Why do you think you might have been fired?

A: I'm very proud that some people think that I'm a danger for the intellectual health of students. When people start thinking of health in intellectual activities, I think there is something wrong. In their opinion I am a dangerous man, since I am a crypto-Marxist, an irrationalist, a nihilist.

Q: From reading *The Order of Things*, one might conclude that individual efforts to reform are impossible because new discoveries have all sorts of meanings and implications their creators never could have understood. In *Discipline and Punish*, for instance, you show that there was a sudden change from the chain gang to the closed police carriage, from the spectacle of punishment to disciplined institutional punishment. But you also point out that this change, which seemed at the time a "reform," was actually only the normalizing of society's ability to punish. So how is conscious change possible?

A: How can you imagine that I think change is impossible since what I have analyzed was always related to political action? All of *Discipline and Punish* is an attempt to answer this question and to show how a new way of thinking took place.

All of us are living and thinking subjects. What I react against is the fact that there is a breach between social history and the history of ideas. Social historians are supposed to describe how people act without thinking, and historians of ideas are supposed to describe how people think without acting. Everybody both acts and thinks. The way people act or react is linked to a way of thinking, and of course thinking is related to tradition. What I have tried to analyze is this very complex phenomenon that made people react in another way to crimes and criminals in a rather short period of time.

I have written two kinds of books. One, *The Order of Things*, is concerned only with scientific thought; the other, *Discipline and Punish*, is concerned with social principles and institutions. History of science doesn't develop in the same way as social sensibility. In order to be recognized as scientific discourse, thought must obey certain criteria. In *Discipline and Punish*, texts, practices, and people struggle against each other.

In my books I have really tried to analyze changes, not in order to find the material causes but to show all the factors that interacted and the reactions of people. I believe in the freedom of people. To the same situation, people react in very different ways.

Q: You conclude *Discipline and Punish* by saying that it will "serve as a background for various studies of normalization and the power of knowledge in modern society." What is the relationship of normalization and the concept of man as the center of knowledge?

A: Through these different practices—psychological, medical, *the 'norm'* penitential, educational—a certain idea or model of humanity was developed, and now this idea of man has become normative, self-evident, and is supposed to be universal. Humanism may not be universal but may be quite relative to a certain situation. What we call humanism has been used by Marxists, liberals, Nazis, Catholics. This does not mean that we have to get rid of what we call human rights or freedom, but that we can't say that freedom or human rights has to be limited at certain frontiers. For instance, if you asked eighty years ago if feminine virtue was part of universal humanism, everyone would have answered yes.

What I am afraid of about humanism is that it presents a certain form of our ethics as a universal model for any kind of freedom. I think that there are more secrets, more possible freedoms, and more inventions in our future than we can imagine in humanism as it is dogmatically represented on every side of the political rainbow: the Left, the Center, the Right.

Q: And this is what is suggested by "Technologies of the Self"?

A: Yes. You said before that you have the feeling that I am unpredictable. That's true. But I sometimes appear to myself much too systematic and rigid.

What I have studied are the three traditional problems: (1) What are the relations we have to truth through scientific knowledge, to those "truth games" which are so important in civilization and in which we are both subject and object? (2) What are the relationships we have to others through those strange strategies and power relationships? And (3) what are the relationships between truth, power, and self?

I would like to finish all this with a question: What could be more classic than these questions and more systematic than the evolution through questions one, two, and three and back to the first? I am just at this point.

Two TECHNOLOGIES OF THE SELF

MICHEL FOUCAULT

I

TECHNOLOGIES OF THE SELF

When I began to study the rules, duties, and prohibitions of sexuality, the interdictions and restrictions associated with it, I was concerned not simply with the acts that were permitted and forbidden but with the feelings represented, the thoughts, the desires one might experience, the drives to seek within the self any hidden feeling, any movement of the soul, any desire disguised under illusory forms. There is a very significant difference between interdictions about sexuality and other forms of interdiction. Unlike other interdictions, sexual interdictions are constantly connected with the obligation to tell the truth about oneself.

Two facts may be objected: first, that confession played an important part in penal and religious institutions for all offenses, not only in sex. But the task of analyzing one's sexual desire is always more important than analyzing any other kind of sin.

I am also aware of the second objection: that sexual behavior more than any other was submitted to very strict rules of secrecy, decency, and modesty so that sexuality is related in a strange and complex way both to verbal prohibition and to the obligation to tell the truth, of hiding what one does, and of deciphering who one is.

The association of prohibition and strong incitations to speak is

a constant feature of our culture. The theme of the renunciation
of the flesh was linked to the confession of the monk to the abbot,
to telling the abbot everything that he had in mind.

I conceived of a rather odd project: not the evolution of sexual
behavior but the projection of a history of the link between the
obligation to tell the truth and the prohibitions against sexuality. I
asked: How had the subject been compelled to decipher himself in
regard to what was forbidden? It is a question of the relation
between asceticism and truth.

Max Weber posed the question: If one wants to behave
rationally and regulate one's action according to true principles,
what part of one's self should one renounce? What is the ascetic *extreme self-denial*
price of reason? To what kind of asceticism should one submit? I
posed the opposite question: How have certain kinds of
interdictions required the price of certain kinds of knowledge
about oneself? What must one know about oneself in order to be
willing to renounce anything?

Thus I arrived at the hermeneutics of technologies of the self in
pagan and early Christian practice. I encountered certain
difficulties in this study because these practices are not well
known. First, Christianity has always been more interested in the
history of its beliefs than in the history of real practices. Second,
such a hermeneutics was never organized into a body of doctrine
like textual hermeneutics. Third, the hermeneutics of the self has
been confused with theologies of the soul—concupiscence, sin,
and the fall from grace. Fourth, a hermeneutics of the self has
been diffused across Western culture through numerous channels
and integrated with various types of attitudes and experience so
that it is difficult to isolate and separate it from our own
spontaneous experiences.

CONTEXT OF STUDY

My objective for more than twenty-five years has been to sketch
out a history of the different ways in our culture that humans

develop knowledge about themselves: economics, biology, psychiatry, medicine, and penology. The main point is not to accept this knowledge at face value but to analyze these so-called sciences as very specific "truth games" related to specific techniques that human beings use to understand themselves.

As a context, we must understand that there are four major types of these "technologies," each a matrix of practical reason: (1) technologies of production, which permit us to produce, transform, or manipulate things; (2) technologies of sign systems, which permit us to use signs, meanings, symbols, or signification; (3) technologies of power, which determine the conduct of individuals and submit them to certain ends or domination, an objectivizing of the subject; (4) technologies of the self, which permit individuals to effect by their own means or with the help of others a certain number of operations on their own bodies and souls, thoughts, conduct, and way of being, so as to transform themselves in order to attain a certain state of happiness, purity, wisdom, perfection, or immortality.

These four types of technologies hardly ever function separately, although each one of them is associated with a certain type of domination. Each implies certain modes of training and modification of individuals, not only in the obvious sense of acquiring certain skills but also in the sense of acquiring certain attitudes. I wanted to show both their specific nature and their constant interaction. For instance, one sees the relation between manipulating things and domination in Karl Marx's *Capital*, where every technique of production requires modification of individual conduct—not only skills but also attitudes.

Usually the first two technologies are used in the study of the sciences and linguistics. It is the last two, the technologies of domination and self, which have most kept my attention. I have attempted a history of the organization of knowledge with respect to both domination and the self. For example, I studied madness not in terms of the criteria of formal sciences but to show how a type of management of individuals inside and outside of asylums was made possible by this strange discourse. This contact between the technologies of domination of others and those of the self I call governmentality.

Perhaps I've insisted too much on the technology of domination and power. I am more and more interested in the interaction between oneself and others and in the technologies of individual domination, the history of how an individual acts upon himself, in the technology of self.

THE DEVELOPMENT OF TECHNOLOGIES OF THE SELF

I wish to sketch out the development of the hermeneutics of the self in two different contexts which are historically contiguous: (1) Greco-Roman philosophy in the first two centuries A.D. of the early Roman Empire and (2) Christian spirituality and the monastic principles developed in the fourth and fifth centuries of the late Roman Empire.

Moreover, I wish to discuss the subject not only in theory but in relation to a set of practices in late antiquity. These practices were constituted in Greek as *epimelēsthai sautou*, "to take care of yourself," "the concern with self," "to be concerned, to take care of yourself."

The precept "to be concerned with oneself" was, for the Greeks, one of the main principles of cities, one of the main rules for social and personal conduct and for the art of life. For us now this notion is rather obscure and faded. When one is asked "What is the most important moral principle in ancient philosophy?" the immediate answer is not "Take care of oneself" but the Delphic principle, *gnothi sauton* ("Know yourself").

Perhaps our philosophical tradition has overemphasized the latter and forgotten the former. The Delphic principle was not an abstract one concerning life; it was technical advice, a rule to be observed for the consultation of the oracle. "Know yourself" meant "Do not suppose yourself to be a god." Other commentators suggest that it meant "Be aware of what you really ask when you come to consult the oracle."

In Greek and Roman texts, the injunction of having to know yourself was always associated with the other principle of having to take care of yourself, and it was that need to care for oneself that brought the Delphic maxim into operation. It is implicit in all Greek and Roman culture and has been explicit since Plato's *Alcibiades I*. In the Socratic dialogues, in Xenophon, Hippocrates, and in the Neoplatonist tradition from Albinus on, one had to be concerned with oneself. One had to occupy oneself with oneself before the Delphic principle was brought into action. There was a subordination of the second principle to the former. I have three or four examples of this.

In Plato's *Apology*, 29^e , Socrates presents himself before his judges as a master of *epimeleia heautou*. You are "not ashamed to care for the acquisition of wealth and for reputation and honor," he tells them, but you do not concern yourselves with yourselves, that is, with "wisdom, truth and the perfection of the soul." He, on the other hand, watches over the citizens to make sure they occupy themselves with themselves.

Socrates says three important things with regard to his invitation to others to occupy themselves with themselves: (1) His mission was conferred on him by the gods, and he won't abandon it except with his last breath. (2) For this task he demands no reward; he is disinterested; he performs it out of benevolence. (3) His mission is useful for the city—more useful than the Athenians' military victory at Olympia—because in teaching people to occupy themselves with themselves, he teaches them to occupy themselves with the city.

Eight centuries later, one finds the same notion and the same phrase in Gregory of Nyssa's treatise, *On Virginity*, but with an entirely different meaning. Gregory did not mean the movement by which one takes care of oneself and the city; he meant the movement by which one renounces the world and marriage and detaches oneself from the flesh and, with virginity of heart and body, recovers the immortality of which one has been deprived. In commenting on the parable of the drachma (Luke 15:8–10), Gregory exhorts one to light the lamp and turn the house over and search, until gleaming in the shadow one sees the drachma within. In order to recover the efficacy which God has printed on one's soul and which the body has tarnished, one must take care of oneself and search every corner of the soul (*De Virg.* 12).

We can see that Christian asceticism, like ancient philosophy, places itself under the same sign of concern with oneself. The obligation to know oneself is one of the elements of its central preoccupation. Between these two extremes—Socrates and Gregory of Nyssa—taking care of oneself constituted not only a principle but also a constant practice.

I have two more examples. The first Epicurean text to serve as a manual of morals was the *Letter to Menoeceus* (Diogenes Laërtius 10.122–38). Epicurus writes that it is never too early, never too late, to occupy oneself with one's soul. One should philosophize when one is young and also when one is old. It was a task to be carried on throughout life. Teachings about everyday life were organized around taking care of oneself in order to help every member of the group with the mutual work of salvation.

Another example comes from an Alexandrian text, *On the Contemplative Life*, by Philo of Alexandria. He describes an obscure, enigmatic group on the periphery of Hellenistic and Hebraic culture called the Therapeutae, marked by its religiosity. It was an austere community, devoted to reading, to healing meditation, to individual and collective prayer, and to meeting for a spiritual banquet (*agapē*, "feast"). These practices stemmed from the principal task, concern for oneself (*De Vita Cont.* 36).

This is the point of departure for some possible analysis for the care of the self in ancient culture. I would like to analyze the relation between care and self-knowledge, the relation found in Greco-Roman and Christian traditions between the care of oneself and the too-well-known principle "Know yourself." As there are different forms of care, there are different forms of self.

SUMMARY

There are several reasons why "Know yourself" has obscured "Take care of yourself." First, there has been a profound transformation in the moral principles of Western society. We find it difficult to base rigorous morality and austere principles on the precept that we should give ourselves more care than anything else in the world. We are more inclined to see taking care of ourselves as an immorality, as a means of escape from all possible rules. We inherit the tradition of Christian morality which makes self-renunciation the condition for salvation. To know oneself was paradoxically the way to self-renunciation.

We also inherit a secular tradition which respects external law as the basis for morality. How then can respect for the self be the basis for morality? We are the inheritors of a social morality which seeks the rules for acceptable behavior in relations with others. Since the sixteenth century, criticism of established morality has been undertaken in the name of the importance of recognizing and knowing the self. Therefore, it is difficult to see concern with oneself as compatible with morality. "Know thyself" has obscured "Take care of yourself" because our morality, a morality of asceticism, insists that the self is that which one can reject.

The second reason is that, in theoretical philosophy from Descartes to Husserl, knowledge of the self (the thinking subject) takes on an ever-increasing importance as the first step in the theory of knowledge.

To summarize: There has been an inversion between the hierarchy of the two principles of antiquity, "Take care of yourself" and "Know thyself." In Greco-Roman culture knowledge of oneself appeared as the consequence of taking care of yourself. In the modern world, knowledge of oneself constitutes the fundamental principle.

II

The first philosophical elaboration of the concern with taking care of oneself that I wish to consider is found in Plato's *Alcibiades I*. The date of its writing is uncertain, and it may be a spurious Platonic dialogue. It is not my intention to study dates but to point out the principal features of the care of self which is the center of the dialogue.

The Neoplatonists in the third or fourth century A.D. show the significance given to this dialogue and the importance it assumed in the classical tradition. They wanted to organize Plato's dialogues as pedagogy and as the matrix for encyclopedic knowledge. They considered *Alcibiades* to be the first dialogue of Plato, the first to be read, the first to be studied. It was *arche*. In the second century Albinus said that every gifted young man who wanted to stand apart from politics and practice virtue should study the *Alcibiades*. It provided the point of departure and a program for all Platonic philosophy. "Taking care of oneself" was its first principle. I would like to analyze the care of self in the *Alcibiades I* in terms of three aspects.

1. How is this question introduced into the dialogue? What are the reasons Alcibiades and Socrates are brought to the notion of taking care of one's self?

Alcibiades is about to begin his public and political life. He wishes to speak before the people and be all-powerful in the city. He is not satisfied with his traditional status, with the privileges of his birth and heritage. He wishes to gain personal power over all others both inside and outside the city. At this point of intersection and transformation, Socrates intervenes and declares his love for Alcibiades. Alcibiades can no longer be the beloved; he must become a lover. He must become active in the political and the love game. Thus, there is a dialectic between political and erotic discourse. Alcibiades makes his transition in specific ways in both politics and love.

An ambivalence is evident in Alcibiades' political and erotic vocabulary. During his adolescence Alcibiades was desirable and had many admirers, but now that his beard is growing, his lovers disappear. Earlier, he had rejected them all in the bloom of his beauty because he wanted to be dominant, not dominated. He did not wish to be dominated in youth, but now he wants to dominate others. This is the moment Socrates appears, and he succeeds where the others have failed: He will make Alcibiades submit, but in a different sense. They make a pact—Alcibiades will submit to his lover, Socrates, not in a physical but in a spiritual sense. The intersection of political ambition and philosophical love is "taking care of oneself."

2. In that relationship, why should Alcibiades be concerned with himself, and why is Socrates concerned with that concern of Alcibiades? Socrates asks Alcibiades about his personal capacity and the nature of his ambition. Does he know the meaning of the rule of law, of justice or concord? Alcibiades clearly knows nothing. Socrates calls upon him to compare his education with that of the Persian and Spartan kings, his rivals. Spartan and Persian princes have teachers in Wisdom, Justice, Temperance, and Courage. By comparison, Alcibiades' education is like that of an old, ignorant slave. He doesn't know these things so he can't apply himself to knowledge. But, says Socrates, it's not too late. To help him gain the upper hand—to acquire *technē*—Alcibiades must apply himself, he must take care of himself. But Alcibiades doesn't know to what he must apply himself. What is this knowledge he seeks? He is embarrassed and confused. Socrates calls upon him to take heart.

In 127^d of the *Alcibiades* we find the first appearance of the phrase, *epimelēsthai sautou*. Concern for self always refers to an active political and erotic state. *Epimelēsthai* expresses something much more serious than the simple fact of paying attention. It involves various things: taking pains with one's holdings and one's health. It is always a real activity and not just an attitude. It is used in reference to the activity of a farmer tending his fields, his cattle, and his house, or to the job of the king in taking care of his city and citizens, or to the worship of ancestors or gods, or as a medical term to signify the fact of caring. It is highly significant that the concern for self in *Alcibiades I* is directly related to a defective pedagogy, one which concerns political ambition and a specific moment of life.

3. The rest of the text is devoted to an analysis of this notion of *epimelēsthai*, "taking pains with oneself." It is divided into two questions: What is this self of which one has to take care, and of what does that care consist?

First, what is the self (129^b)? Self is a reflexive pronoun, and it has two meanings. *Auto* means "the same," but it also conveys the notion of identity. The latter meaning shifts the question from "What is this self?" to "What is the plateau on which I shall find my identity?"

Alcibiades tries to find the self in a dialectical movement. When you take care of the body, you don't take care of the self. The self is not clothing, tools, or possessions. It is to be found in the principle which uses these tools, a principle not of the body but of the soul. You have to worry about your soul—that is the principal activity of caring for yourself. The care of the self is the care of the activity and not the care of the soul-as-substance.

The second question is: How must we take care of this principle of activity, the soul? Of what does this care consist? One must know of what the soul consists. The soul cannot know itself except by looking at itself in a similar element, a mirror. Thus, it must contemplate the divine element. In this divine contemplation, the soul will be able to discover rules to serve as a basis for just behavior and political action. The effort of the soul to know itself is the principle on which just political action can be founded, and Alcibiades will be a good politician insofar as he contemplates his soul in the divine element.

Often the discussion gravitates around and is phrased in terms of the Delphic principle, "Know yourself." To take care of oneself consists of knowing oneself. Knowing oneself becomes the object of the quest of concern for self. Being occupied with oneself and political activities are linked. The dialogue ends when Alcibiades knows he must take care of himself by examining his soul.

This early text illuminates the historical background of the precept "taking care of oneself" and sets out four main problems that endure throughout antiquity, although the solutions offered often differ from those in Plato's *Alcibiades*.

First, there is the problem of the relation between being occupied with oneself and political activity. In the later Hellenistic and imperial periods, the question is presented in an alternative way: When is it better to turn away from political activity to concern oneself with oneself?

Second, there is the problem of the relationship between being occupied with oneself and pedagogy. For Socrates, occupying oneself with oneself is the duty of a young man, but later in the Hellenistic period it is seen as the permanent duty of one's whole life.

Third, there is the problem of the relationship between concern for oneself and the knowledge of oneself. Plato gave priority to the Delphic maxim, "Know yourself." The privileged position of "Know yourself" is characteristic of all Platonists. Later, in the Hellenistic and Greco-Roman periods, this is reversed. The accent was not on the knowledge of self but on the concern with oneself. The latter was given an autonomy and even a preeminence as a philosophical issue.

Fourth, there is the problem of the relationship between the care of self and philosophical love, or the relation to a master.

In the Hellenistic and imperial periods, the Socratic notion of "taking care of oneself" became a common, universal philosophical theme. "Care of the self" was accepted by Epicurus and his followers, by the Cynics, and by such Stoics as Seneca, Rufus, and Galen. The Pythagoreans gave attention to the notion of an ordered life in common. This theme of taking care of oneself was not abstract advice but a widespread activity, a network of obligations and services to the soul. Following Epicurus himself, the Epicureans believed that it's never too late to occupy oneself with oneself. The Stoics say you must attend to the self, "retire into the self and stay there." Lucian parodied the notion. It was an extremely widespread activity, and it brought about competition between the rhetoricians and those who turned toward themselves, particularly over the question of the role of the master.

There were charlatans, of course. But certain individuals took it seriously. It was generally acknowledged that it was good to be reflective, at least briefly. Pliny advises a friend to set aside a few moments a day, or several weeks or months, for a retreat into himself. This was an active leisure—to study, to read, to prepare for misfortune or death. It was a meditation and a preparation.

Writing was also important in the culture of taking care of oneself. One of the main features of taking care involved taking notes on oneself to be reread, writing treatises and letters to friends to help them, and keeping notebooks in order to reactivate for oneself the truths one needed. Seneca's letters are an example of this self-exercise.

In traditional political life, oral culture was largely dominant, and therefore rhetoric was important. But the development of the administrative structures and the bureaucracy of the imperial period increased the amount and role of writing in the political sphere. In Plato's writings, dialogue gave way to the literary pseudodialogue. But by the Hellenistic age, writing prevailed, and real dialectic passed to correspondence. Taking care of oneself became linked to constant writing activity. The self is something to write about, a theme or object (subject) of writing activity. That is not a modern trait born of the Reformation or of romanticism; it is one of the most ancient Western traditions. It was well established and deeply rooted when Augustine started his *Confessions*.

The new concern with self involved a new experience of self. The new form of the experience of the self is to be seen in the first and second century when introspection becomes more and more detailed. A relation developed between writing and vigilance. Attention was paid to nuances of life, mood, and reading, and the experience of oneself was intensified and widened by virtue of this act of writing. A whole field of experience opened which earlier was absent.

One can compare Cicero to the later Seneca or Marcus Aurelius. We see, for example, Seneca's and Marcus's meticulous concern with the details of daily life, with the movements of the spirit, with self-analysis. Everything in the imperial period is present in Marcus Aurelius's letter of 144–45 A.D. to Fronto:

Hail, my sweetest of masters.

We are well. I slept somewhat late owing to my slight cold, which seems now to have subsided. So from five A.M. till 9, I spent the time partly in reading some of Cato's *Agriculture*, partly in writing not quite such wretched stuff, by heavens, as yesterday. Then, after paying my respects to my father, I relieved my throat, I will not say by gargling—though the word *gargarisso* is, I believe, found in Novius and elsewhere— but by swallowing honey water as far as the gullet and ejecting it again. After easing my throat I went off to my father and attended him at a sacrifice. Then we went to luncheon. What do you think I ate? A wee bit of bread, though I saw others devouring beans, onions, and herrings full of roe. We then worked hard at grape-gathering, and had a good sweat, and were merry and, as the poet says, "still left some clusters hanging high as gleanings of the vintage." After six o'clock we came home.

I did but little work and that to no purpose. Then I had a long chat with my little mother as she sat on the bed. My talk was this: "What do you think my Fronto is now doing?" Then she: "And what do you think my Gratia is doing?" Then I: "And what do you think our little sparrow, the wee Gratia, is doing?" Whilst we were chattering in this way and disputing which of us two loved the one or other of you two the better, the gong sounded, an intimation that my father had gone to his bath. So we had supper after we had bathed in the oil-press room; I do not mean bathed in the oil-press room, but when we had bathed, had supper there, and we enjoyed hearing the yokels chaffing one another. After coming back, before I turn over and snore, I get my task done and give my dearest of masters an account of the day's doings, and if I could miss him more, I would not grudge wasting away a little more. Farewell, my Fronto, wherever you are, most honey-sweet, my love, my delight. How is it between you and me? I love you and you are away.

This letter presents a description of everyday life. All the details of taking care of oneself are here, all the unimportant things he has done. Cicero tells only important things, but in Aurelius's letter these details are important because they are you—what you thought, what you felt.

The relation between the body and the soul is interesting too. For the Stoics, the body was not so important, but Marcus Aurelius speaks of himself, his health, what he has eaten, his sore throat. That is quite characteristic of the ambiguity about the body in this cultivation of the self. Theoretically, the culture is soul-oriented, but all the concerns of the body take on a huge importance. In Pliny and Seneca there is great hypochondria. They retreat to a house in the countryside. They have intellectual activities but rural activities as well. They eat and engage in the activity of peasants. The importance of the rural retreat in this letter is that nature helps put one in contact with oneself.

There is also a love relationship with Aurelius and Fronto, one between a twenty-four-year-old and a forty-year-old man. *Ars erotica* is a theme of discussion. Homosexual love was important in this period and carried over into Christian monasticism.

Finally, in the last lines, there is an allusion to the examination of conscience at the end of the day. Aurelius goes to bed and looks in the notebook to see what he was going to do and how it corresponds to what he did. The letter is the transcription of that examination of conscience. It stresses what you did, not what you thought. That is the difference between practice in the Hellenistic and imperial periods and later monastic practice. In Seneca too there are only deeds, not thoughts. But it does prefigure Christian confession.

This genre of epistles shows a side apart from the philosophy of the era. The examination of conscience begins with this letter writing. Diary writing comes later. It dates from the Christian Era and focuses on the notion of the struggle of the soul.

III

In my discussion of Plato's *Alcibiades*, I have isolated three major themes: first, the relation between care for oneself and care for the political life; second, the relation between taking care of the self and defective education; and third, the relation between taking care of oneself and knowing oneself. Whereas we saw in the *Alcibiades* the close relation between "Take care of yourself" and "Know yourself," taking care of yourself eventually became absorbed in knowing yourself.

We can see these three themes in Plato, also in the Hellenistic period, and four to five centuries later in Seneca, Plutarch, Epictetus, and the like. If the problems are the same, the solutions and themes are quite different and, in some cases, the opposite of the Platonic meanings.

First, to be concerned with self in the Hellenistic and Roman periods is not exclusively a preparation for political life. Care of the self has become a universal principle. One must leave politics to take better care of the self.

Second, the concern with oneself is not just obligatory for young people concerned with their education; it is a way of living for everybody throughout their lives.

Third, even if self-knowledge plays an important role in taking care of oneself, it involves other relationships as well.

I want to discuss briefly the first two points: the universality of the care of the self independent of political life, and the care of the self throughout one's life.

1. A medical model was substituted for Plato's pedagogical model. The care of the self isn't another kind of pedagogy; it has to become permanent medical care. Permanent medical care is one of the central features of the care of the self. One must become the doctor of oneself.

2. Since we have to take care throughout life, the objective is no longer to get prepared for adult life, or for another life, but to get prepared for a certain complete achievement of life. This achievement is complete at the moment just prior to death. This notion of a happy proximity to death— of old age as completion—is an inversion of the traditional Greek values on youth.

3. Lastly, we have the various practices to which cultivation of self has given rise and the relation of self-knowledge to these.

In *Alcibiades I*, the soul had a mirror relation to itself, which relates to the concept of memory and justifies dialogue as a method of discovering truth in the soul. But, from the time of Plato to the Hellenistic age, the relationship between care of the self and knowledge of the self changed. We may note two perspectives.

In the philosophical movements of Stoicism in the imperial period there is a different conception of truth and memory, and another method of examining the self. First, we see the disappearence of dialogue and the increasing importance of a new pedagogical relationship—a new pedagogical game where the master/teacher speaks and doesn't ask questions and the disciple doesn't answer but must listen and keep silent. A culture of silence becomes more and more important. In Pythagorean culture, disciples kept silent for five years as a pedagogical rule. They didn't ask questions or speak up during the lesson, but they developed the art of listening. This is the positive condition for acquiring truth. The tradition is picked up during the imperial period, where we see the beginning of the culture of silence and the art of listening rather than the cultivation of dialogue as in Plato.

To learn the art of listening, we have to read Plutarch's treatise on the art of listening to lectures (*Peri tou akouein*). At the beginning of this treatise, Plutarch says that, following schooling, we have to learn to listen to *logos* throughout our adult life. The art of listening is crucial so you can tell what is true and what is dissimulation, what is rhetorical truth and what is falsehood in the discourse of the rhetoricians. Listening is linked to the fact that you're not under the control of the masters but you must listen to *logos*. You keep silent at the lecture. You think about it afterward. This is the art of listening to the voice of the master and the voice of reason in yourself.

The advice may seem banal, but I think it's important. In his treatise *On the Contemplative Life*, Philo of Alexandria describes banquets of silence, not debauched banquets with wine, boys, revelry, and dialogue. There is instead a teacher who gives a monologue on the interpretation of the Bible and a very precise indication of the way people must listen (*De Vita Cont.* 77). For example, they must always assume the same posture when listening. The morphology of this notion is an interesting theme in monasticism and pedagogy henceforth.

In Plato the themes of contemplation of self and care of self are related dialectically through dialogue. Now in the imperial period we have the themes of, on one side, the obligation of listening to truth and, on the other side, of looking and listening to the self for the truth within. The difference between the one era and the other is one of the great signs of the disappearance of the dialectical structure.

What was an examination of conscience in this culture, and how does one look at oneself? For the Pythagoreans, the examination of conscience had to do with purification. Since sleep was related to death as a kind of encounter with the gods, you had to purify yourself before going to sleep. Remembering the dead was an exercise for the memory. But in the Hellenistic and the early imperial periods, you see this practice acquiring new values and signification. There are several relevant texts: Seneca's *De Ira*, and *De Tranquilitate* and the beginning of Marcus Aurelius's fourth book of *Meditations*.

Seneca's *De Ira* (book 3) contains some traces of the old tradition. He describes an examination of conscience. The same thing was recommended by the Epicureans, and the practice was rooted in the Pythagorean tradition. The goal was the purification of the conscience using a mnemonic device. Do good things, have a good examination of the self, and a good sleep follows together with good dreams, which is contact with the gods.

Seneca seems to use juridical language, and it seems that the self is both the judge and the accused. Seneca is the judge and prosecutes the self so that the examination is a kind of trial. But if you look closer, it's rather different from a court. Seneca uses terms related not to juridical but to administrative practices, as when a comptroller looks at the books or when a building inspector examines a building. Self-examination is taking stock. Faults are simply good intentions left undone. The rule is a means of doing something correctly, not judging what has happened in the past. Later, Christian confession will look for bad intentions.

It is this administrative view of his own life much more than the juridical model that is important. Seneca isn't a judge who has to punish but a stock-taking administrator. He is a permanent administrator of himself, not a judge of his past. He sees that everything has been done correctly following the rule but not the law. It is not real faults for which he reproaches himself but rather his lack of success. His errors are of strategy, not of moral character. He wants to make adjustments between what he wanted to do and what he had done and reactivate the rules of conduct, not excavate his guilt. In Christian confession, the penitent is obliged to memorize laws but does so in order to discover his sins.

For Seneca it isn't a question of discovering truth in the subject but of remembering truth, recovering a truth which has been forgotten. Second, the subject doesn't forget himself, his nature, origin, or his supernatural affinity, but the rules of conduct, what he ought to have done. Third, the recollection of errors committed in the day measures the distinction between what has been done and what should have been done. Fourth, the subject is not the operating ground for the process of deciphering but is the point where rules of conduct come together in memory. The subject constitutes the intersection between acts which have to be regulated and rules for what ought to be done. This is quite different from the Platonic conception and from the Christian conception of conscience.

The Stoics spiritualized the notion of *anachoresis*, the retreat of an army, the hiding of an escaped slave from his master, or the retreat into the country away from the towns, as in Marcus Aurelius's country retreat. A retreat into the country becomes a spiritual retreat into oneself. It is a general attitude and also a precise act every day; you retire into the self to discover—but not to discover faults and deep feelings, only to remember rules of action, the main laws of behavior. It is a mnemotechnical formula.

IV

I have spoken of three Stoic techniques of self: letters to friends and disclosure of self; examination of self and conscience, including a review of what was done, of what should have been done, and comparison of the two. Now I want to consider the third Stoic technique, *askēsis*, not a disclosure of the secret self but a remembering.

For Plato, one must discover the truth that is within one. For the Stoics, truth is not in oneself but in the *logoi*, the teaching of the teachers. One memorizes what one has heard, converting the statements one hears into rules of conduct. The subjectivization of truth is the aim of these techniques. During the imperial period, one couldn't assimilate ethical principles without a theoretical framework such as science, as for example in Lucretius's *De Rerum Naturae*. There are structural questions underlying the practice of the examination of the self every night. I want to underscore the fact that in Stoicism it's not the deciphering of the self, not the means to disclose secrecy, which is important; it's the memory of what you've done and what you've had to do.

In Christianity asceticism always refers to a certain renunciation of the self and of reality because most of the time your self is a part of that reality you have to renounce in order to get access to another level of reality. This move to attain the renunciation of the self distinguishes Christian asceticism.

In the philosophical tradition dominated by Stoicism, *askēsis* means not renunciation but the progressive consideration of self, or mastery over oneself, obtained not through the renunciation of reality but through the acquisition and assimilation of truth. It has as its final aim not preparation for another reality but access to the reality of this world. The Greek word for this is *paraskeuazō* ("to get prepared"). It is a set of practices by which one can acquire, assimilate, and transform truth into a permanent principle of action. *Aletheia* becomes *ethos*. It is a process of becoming more subjective.

What are the principle features of *askēsis*? They include exercises in which the subject puts himself in a situation in which he can verify whether he can confront events and use the discourses with which he is armed. It is a question of testing the preparation. Is this truth assimilated enough to become ethics so that we can behave as we must when an event presents itself?

The Greeks characterized the two poles of those exercises by the terms *meletē* and *gymnasia*. *Meletē* means "meditation," according to the Latin translation, *meditatio*. It has the same root as *epimelēsthai*. It is a rather vague term, a technical term borrowed from rhetoric. *Meletē* is the work one undertook in order to prepare a discourse or an improvisation by thinking over useful terms and arguments. You had to anticipate the real situation through dialogue in your thoughts. The philosophical meditation is this kind of meditation: It is composed of memorizing responses and reactivating those memories by placing oneself in a situation where one can imagine how one would react. One judges the reasoning one should use in an imaginary exercise ("Let us suppose . . .") in order to test an action or event (for example, "How would I react?"). Imagining the articulation of possible events to test how you would react—that's meditation.

The most famous exercise of meditation is the *premeditatio mallorum* as practiced by the Stoics. It is an ethical, imaginary experience. In appearance it's a rather dark and pessimistic vision of the future. You can compare it to what Husserl says about eidetic reduction.

The Stoics developed three eidetic reductions of future misfortune. First, it is not a question of imagining the future as it is likely to turn out but to imagine the worst which can happen, even if there's little chance that it will turn out that way—the worst as certainty, as actualizing what could happen, not as calculation of probability. Second, one shouldn't envisage things as possibly taking place in the distant future but as already actual and in the process of taking place. For example, imagining not that one might be exiled but rather that one is already exiled, subjected to torture, and dying. Third, one does this not in order to experience inarticulate sufferings but in order to convince oneself that they are not real ills. The reduction of all that is possible, of all the duration and of all the misfortunes, reveals not something bad but what we have to accept. It consists of having at the same time the future and the present event. The Epicureans were hostile to it because they thought it was useless. They thought it was better to recollect and memorize past pleasures in order to derive pleasure from present events.

At the opposite pole is *gymnasia* ("to train oneself"). While *meditatio* is an imaginary experience that trains thought, *gymnasia* is training in a real situation, even if it's been artificially induced. There is a long tradition behind this: sexual abstinence, physical privation, and other rituals of purification.

Those practices of abstinence have other meanings than purification or witnessing demonic force, as in Pythagoras and Socrates. In the culture of the Stoics, their function is to establish and test the independence of the individual with regard to the external world. For example, in Plutarch's *De Genio Socratis*, one gives oneself over to very hard sporting activities. Or one tempts oneself by placing oneself in front of many tantalizing dishes and then renouncing these appetizing dishes. Then you call your slaves and give them the dishes, and you take the meal prepared for the slaves. Another example is Seneca's eighteenth letter to Lucilius. He prepares for a great feast day by acts of mortification of the flesh in order to convince himself that poverty is not an evil and that he can endure it.

Between these poles of training in thought and training in reality, *meletē* and *gymnasia*, there are a whole series of intermediate possibilities. Epictetus provides the best example of the middle ground between these poles. He wants to watch perpetually over representations, a technique which culminates in Freud. There are two metaphors important from his point of view: the night watchman, who doesn't admit anyone into town if that person can't prove who he is (we must be "watchman" over the flux of thought), and the money changer, who verifies the authenticity of currency, looks at it, weighs and verifies it. We have to be money changers of our own representations of our thoughts, vigilantly testing them, verifying them, their metal, weight, effigy.

The same metaphor of the money changer is found in the Stoics and in early Christian literature but with different meanings. When Epictetus says you have to be a money changer, he means as soon as an idea comes to mind you have to think of the rules you must apply to evaluate it. For John Cassian, being a money changer and looking at your thoughts means something very different: It means you must try to decipher if, at the root of the movement which brings you the representations, there is or is not concupiscence or desire—if your innocent thought has evil origins; if you have something underlying which is the great seducer, which is perhaps hidden, the money of your thought.

In Epictetus there are two exercises: sophistic and ethical. The first are exercises borrowed from school: question-and-answer games. This must be an ethical game; that is, it must teach a moral lesson. The second are ambulatory exercises. In the morning you go for a walk, and you test your reactions to that walk. The purpose of both exercises is control of representations, not the deciphering of truth. They are reminders about conforming to the rules in the face of adversity. A pre-Freudian machine of censorship is described word for word in the tests of Epictetus and Cassian. For Epictetus, the control of representations means not deciphering but recalling principles of acting and thus seeing, through self-examination, if they govern your life. It is a kind of permanent self-examination. You have to be your own censor. The meditation on death is the culmination of all these exercises.

In addition to letters, examination, and *askēsis*, we must now evoke a fourth technique in the examination of the self, the interpretation of dreams. It was to have an important destiny in the nineteenth century, but it occupied a relatively marginal position in the ancient world. Philosophers had an ambivalent attitude toward the interpretation of dreams. Most Stoics are critical and skeptical about such interpretation. But there is still the popular and general practice of it. There were experts who were able to interpret dreams, including Pythagoras and some of the Stoics, and some experts who wrote books to teach people to interpret their own dreams. There were huge amounts of literature on how to do it, but the only surviving dream manual is *The Interpretation of Dreams* by Artemidorus (second century A.D.). Dream interpretation was important because in antiquity the meaning of a dream was an announcement of a future event.

I should mention two other documents dealing with the importance of dream interpretation for everyday life. The first is by Synesius of Cyrene in the fourth century A.D. He was well known and cultivated. Even though he was not a Christian, he asked to be a bishop. His remarks on dreams are interesting, for public divination was forbidden in order to spare the emperor bad news. Therefore, one had to interpret one's own dreams; one had to be a self-interpreter. To do it, one had to remember not only one's own dreams but the events before and after. One had to record what happened every day, both the life of the day and the life of the night.

Aelius Aristides' *Sacred Discourses*, written in the second century, records his dreams and explains how to interpret them. He believed that in the interpretation of dreams we receive advice from the gods about remedies for illness. With this work, we are at the crossing point of two kinds of discourses. It isn't the writing of self's daily activities that is the matrix of the *Sacred Discourses* but the ritual inscription of praises to the gods that have healed one.

V

I wish to examine the scheme of one of the main techniques of the self in early Christianity and what it was as a truth game. To do so, I must look at the transition from pagan to Christian culture in which it is possible to see clear-cut continuities and discontinuities.

Christianity belongs to the salvation religions. It's one of those religions which is supposed to lead the individual from one reality to another, from death to life, from time to eternity. In order to achieve that, Christianity imposed a set of conditions and rules of behavior for a certain transformation of the self.

Christianity is not only a salvation religion, it's a confessional religion. It imposes very strict obligations of truth, dogma, and canon, more so than do the pagan religions. Truth obligations to believe this or that were and are still very numerous. The duty to accept a set of obligations, to hold certain books as permanent truth, to accept authoritarian decisions in matters of truth, not only to believe certain things but to show that one believes, and to accept institutional authority are all characteristic of Christianity.

Christianity requires another form of truth obligation different from faith. Each person has the duty to know who he is, that is, to try to know what is happening inside him, to acknowledge faults, to recognize temptations, to locate desires, and everyone is obliged to disclose these things either to God or to others in the community and hence to bear public or private witness against oneself. The truth obligations of faith and the self are linked together. This link permits a purification of the soul impossible without self-knowledge.

It's not the same in the Catholic as in the Reform tradition. But the main features of both are an ensemble of truth obligations dealing with faith, books, dogma, and one dealing with truth, heart, and soul. Access to truth cannot be conceived of without purity of the soul. Purity of the soul is the consequence of self-knowledge and a condition for understanding the text; in Augustine: *Quis facit veritatem* (to make truth in oneself, to get access to the light).

I'd like to analyze the ways by which, in order to get access to the light, the church conceived of illumination: the disclosure of the self. The sacrament of penance and the confession of sins are rather late innovations. Christians of the first centuries had different forms for discovering and deciphering truth about themselves. One of the two main forms of those disclosures can be characterized by the word *exomologēsis*, or "recognition of fact." Even the Latin fathers used this Greek term with no exact translation. For Christians it meant to recognize publicly the truth of their faith or to recognize publicly that they were Christians.

The word also had a penitential meaning. When a sinner seeks penance, he must visit the bishop and ask for it. In early Christianity, penitence was not an act or a ritual but a status imposed on somebody who had committed very serious sins.

Exomologēsis was a ritual of recognizing oneself as a sinner and penitent. It had several characteristics. First, you were a penitent for four to ten years, and this status affected your life. There was fasting, and there were rules about clothing and prohibitions about sex. The individual was marked so he couldn't live the same life as others. Even after his reconciliation, he suffered from a number of prohibitions; for example, he could not marry or become a priest.

Within this status you find the obligation of *exomologēsis*. The sinner seeks his penance. He visits the bishop and asks the bishop to impose on him the status of a penitent. He must explain why he wants the status, and he has to explain his faults. This was not a confession; it was a condition of the status. Later, in the medieval period, *exomologēsis* became a ritual which took place at the end of the period of penance just before reconciliation. This ceremony placed him among the other Christians. Of this recognition ceremony, Tertullian says that wearing a hair shirt and ashes, wretchedly dressed, the sinner stands humbled before the church. Then he prostrates himself and kisses the brethren's knees (*On Repentance* 9–12). *Exomologēsis* is not a verbal behavior but the dramatic recognition of one's status as a penitent. Much

later, in the *Epistles* of Jerome, there is a description of the
penitence of Fabiola, a Roman lady. During these days, Fabiola
was in the ranks of penitents. People wept with her, lending
drama to her public chastisement.

Recognition also designates the entire process that the penitent
experiences in this status over the years. He is the aggregate of
manifested penitential behavior, of self-punishment as well as of
self-revelation. The acts by which he punishes himself are
indistinguishable from the acts by which he reveals himself.
Self-punishment and the voluntary expression of the self are
bound together. This link is evident in many writings. Cyprian,
for example, talks of exhibitions of shame and modesty. Penance
is not nominal but dramatic.

To prove suffering, to show shame, to make visible humility and
exhibit modesty—these are the main features of punishment.
Penitence in early Christianity is a way of life acted out at all times
by accepting the obligation to disclose oneself. It must be visibly
represented and accompanied by others who recognize the ritual.
This approach endured until the fifteenth and sixteenth centuries.

Tertullian uses the term *publicatio sui* to characterize *exomologēsis*.
Publicatio sui is related to Seneca's daily self-examination, which
was, however, completely private. For Seneca, *exomologēsis* or
publicatio sui doesn't imply verbal analysis of deeds or thoughts; it
is only a somatic and symbolic expression. What was private for
the Stoics was public for the Christians.

What were its functions? First, this publication was a way to
rub out sin and to restore the purity acquired by baptism.
Second, it was also to show a sinner as he is. That's the paradox
at the heart of *exomologēsis;* it rubs out the sin and yet reveals the
sinner. The greater part of the act of penitence was not telling the
truth of sin but showing the true sinful being of the sinner. It was
not a way for the sinner to explain his sins but a way to present
himself as a sinner.

Why should showing forth efface the sins? Exposé is the heart
of *exomologēsis*. In the Christianity of the first centuries, Christian

authors had recourse to three models to explain the relation between the paradox of rubbing out sins and disclosing oneself.

The first is the medical model: One must show one's wounds in order to be cured. Another model, which was less frequent, was the tribunal model of judgment. One always appeases one's judge by confessing faults. The sinner plays devil's advocate, as will the devil on the Day of Judgment.

The most important model used to explain *exomologēsis* was the model of death, of torture, or of martyrdom. The theories and practices of penance were elaborated around the problem of the man who prefers to die rather than to compromise or abandon the faith. The way the martyr faces death is the model for the penitent. For the relapsed to be reintegrated into the church, he must expose himself voluntarily to ritual martyrdom. Penance is the affect of change, of rupture with self, past, and world. It's a way to show that you are able to renounce life and self, to show that you can face and accept death. Penitence of sin doesn't have as its target the establishing of an identity but serves instead to mark the refusal of the self, the breaking away from self: *Ego non sum, ego.* This formula is at the heart of *publicatio sui*. It represents a break with one's past identity. These ostentatious gestures have the function of showing the truth of the state of being of the sinner. Self-revelation is at the same time self-destruction.

The difference between the Stoic and Christian traditions is that in the Stoic tradition examination of self, judgment, and discipline show the way to self-knowledge by superimposing truth about self through memory, that is, by memorizing the rules. In *exomologēsis*, the penitent superimposes truth about self by violent rupture and dissociation. It is important to emphasize that this *exomologēsis* is not verbal. It is symbolic, ritual, and theatrical.

VI

During the fourth century we find a very different technology for the disclosure of the self, *exagoreusis*, much less famous than *exomologēsis* but more important. This one is reminiscent of the verbalizing exercises in relation to a teacher/master of the pagan philosophical schools. We can see the transfer of several Stoic technologies of the self to Christian spiritual techniques.

At least one example of self-examination, proposed by John Chrysostom, was exactly the same form and the same administrative character as that described by Seneca in *De Ira*. In the morning we must take account of our expenses, and in the evening we must ask ourselves to render account of our conduct of ourselves, to examine what is to our advantage and what is prejudicial against us, with prayers instead of indiscreet words. That is exactly the Senecan style of self-examination. It's also important to note that this self-examination is rare in Christian literature.

The well-developed and elaborated practice of the self-examination in monastic Christianity is different from the Senecan self-examination and very different from Chrysostom and from *exomologēsis*. This new kind of practice must be understood from the point of view of two principles of Christian spirituality: obedience and contemplation.

In Seneca, the relationship of the disciple with the master was important, but it was instrumental and professional. It was founded on the capacity of the master to lead the disciple to a happy and autonomous life through good advice. The relationship would end when the disciple got access to that life.

For a long series of reasons, obedience has a very different character in monastic life. It differs from the Greco-Roman type of relation to the master in the sense that obedience isn't based just upon a need for self-improvement but must bear on all aspects of a monk's life. There is no element in the life of the monk which may escape from this fundamental and permanent relation of total obedience to the master. John Cassian repeats an old principle from the oriental tradition: "Everything the monk does without permission of his master constitutes a theft." Here obedience is complete control of behavior by the master, not a final autonomous state. It is a sacrifice of the self, of the subject's own will. This is the new technology of the self.

The monk must have the permission of his director to do anything, even die. Everything he does without permission is stealing. There is not a single moment when the monk can be autonomous. Even when he becomes a director himself, he must retain the spirit of obedience. He must keep the spirit of obedience as a permanent sacrifice of the complete control of behavior by the master. The self must constitute self through obedience.

The second feature of monastic life is that contemplation is considered the supreme good. It is the obligation of the monk to turn his thoughts continuously to that point which is God and to make sure that his heart is pure enough to see God. The goal is permanent contemplation of God.

The technology of the self, which developed from obedience and contemplation in the monastery, presents some peculiar characteristics. Cassian gives a rather clear exposition of this technology of the self, a principle of self-examination which he borrowed from the Syrian and Egyptian monastic traditions.

This technology of self-examination of Oriental origins, dominated by obedience and contemplation, is much more concerned with thought than with action. Seneca had placed his stress on action. With Cassian the object is not past actions of the day; it's the present thoughts. Since the monk must continuously turn his thoughts toward God, he must scrutinize the actual course of this thought. This scrutiny thus has as its object the permanent discrimination between thoughts which lead toward God and those which don't. This continual concern with the present is different from the Senecan memorization of deeds and their correspondence with rules. It is what the Greeks referred to with a pejorative word: *logismoi* ("cogitations, reasoning, calculating thought").

There is an etymology of *logismoi* in Cassian, but I don't know if it's sound: *co-agitationes*. The spirit is *polukinetos*, "perpetually moving" (*First Conference of Abbot Serenus* 4). In Cassian, perpetual mobility of spirit is the spirit's weakness. It distracts one from contemplation of God (*First Conference of Abbot Nesterus* 13).

The scrutiny of conscience consists of trying to immobilize consciousness, to eliminate movements of the spirit that divert one from God. That means we have to examine any thought which presents itself to consciousness to see the relation between act and thought, truth and reality, to see if there is anything in this thought which will move our spirit, provoke our desire, turn our spirit away from God. The scrutiny is based on the idea of a secret concupiscence.

There are three major types of self-examination: first, self-examination with respect to thoughts in correspondence to reality (Cartesian); second, self-examination with respect to the way our thoughts relate to rules (Senecan), third, the examination of self with respect to the relation between the hidden thought and an inner impurity. At this moment begins the Christian hermeneutics of the self with its deciphering of inner thoughts. It implies that there is something hidden in ourselves and that we are always in a self-illusion which hides the secret.

In order to make this kind of scrutiny, Cassian says we have to care for ourselves, to attest to our thoughts directly. He gives three analogies. First is the analogy of the mill (*First Conference of Abbot Moses* 18). Thoughts are like grains, and consciousness is the mill store. It is our role as the miller to sort out amongst the grains those which are bad and those which can be admitted to the mill store to give the good flour and good bread of our salvation.

Second, Cassian makes military analogies (*First Conference of Abbot Serenus* 5). He uses an analogy of the officer who orders the good soldiers to march to the right, the bad to the left. We must act like officers who divide soldiers into two files, the good and the bad.

Third, he uses the analogy of a money changer (*First Conference of Abbot Moses* 20–22). Conscience is the money changer of the self. It must examine coins, their effigy, their metal, where they came from. It must weigh them to see if they have been ill used. As there is the image of the emperor on money, so must the image of God be on our thoughts. We must verify the quality of the thought: This effigy of God, is it real? What is its degree of purity? Is it mixed with desire or concupiscence? Thus, we find the same image as in Seneca, but with a different meaning.

Since we have as our role to be a permanent money changer of ourselves, how is it possible to make this discrimination and recognize if a thought is of good quality? How can this "discrimination" actively be done? There is only one way: to tell all thoughts to our director, to be obedient to our master in all things, to engage in the permanent verbalization of all our thoughts. In Cassian, self-examination is subordinated to obedience and the permanent verbalization of thoughts. Neither is true of Stoicism. By telling himself not only his thoughts but also the smallest movements of consciousness, his intentions, the monk stands in a hermeneutic relation not only to the master but to himself. This verbalization is the touchstone or the money of thought.

Why is confession able to assume this hermeneutical role? How can we be the hermeneuts of ourselves in speaking and transcribing all of our thoughts? Confession permits the master to know because of his greater experience and wisdom and therefore to give better advice. Even if the master, in his role as a discriminating power, doesn't say anything, the fact that the thought has been expressed will have an effect of discrimination.

Cassian gives an example of the monk who stole bread. At first he can't tell. The difference between good and evil thoughts is that evil thoughts can't be expressed without difficulty, for evil is hidden and unstated. Because evil thoughts cannot be expressed without difficulty and shame, the cosmological difference between light and dark, between verbalization and sin, secrecy and silence, between God and the devil, may not emerge. Then the monk prostrates himself and confesses. Only when he confesses verbally does the devil go out of him. The verbal expression is the crucial moment (*Second Conference of Abbot Moses* II). Confession is a mark of truth. This idea of the permanent verbal is only an ideal. It is never completely possible. But the price of the permanent verbal was to make everything that couldn't be expressed into a sin.

In conclusion, in the Christianity of the first centuries, there are two main forms of disclosing self, of showing the truth about oneself. The first is *exomologēsis*, or a dramatic expression of the situation of the penitent as sinner which makes manifest his status as sinner. The second is what was called in the spiritual literature *exagoreusis*. This is an analytical and continual verbalization of thoughts carried on in the relation of complete obedience to someone else. This relation is modeled on the renunciation of one's own will and of one's own self.

There is a great difference between *exomologēsis* and *exagoreusis*; yet we have to underscore the fact that there is one important element in common: You cannot disclose without renouncing. *Exomologēsis* had as its model martyrdom. In *exomologeusis*, the sinner had to "kill" himself through ascetic macerations. Whether through martyrdom or through obedience to a master, disclosure of self is the renunciation of one's own self. In *exagorēsis*, on the other hand, you show that, in permanently verbalizing your thoughts and permanently obeying the master, you are renouncing your will and yourself. This practice continues from the beginning of Christianity to the seventeenth century. The inauguration of penance in the thirteenth century is an important step in its rise.

This theme of self-renunciation is very important. Throughout Christianity there is a correlation between disclosure of the self, dramatic or verbalized, and the renunciation of self. My hypothesis from looking at these two techniques is that it's the second one, verbalization, which becomes the more important.

From the eighteenth century to the present, the techniques of verbalization have been reinserted in a different context by the so-called human sciences in order to use them without renunciation of the self but to constitute, positively, a new self. To use these techniques without renouncing oneself constitutes a decisive break.

Three TECHNOLOGIES OF THE SELF

AND SELF-KNOWLEDGE IN THE

SYRIAN THOMAS TRADITION

LUTHER H. MARTIN

In studying both the most admired and the most detested figures in any
society, we can see, as seldom through other evidence, the nature of the
average man's expectations and hopes for himself.[1]

The understanding of a Hellenistic period of history, since its first
delineation by J. G. Droysen in the mid-nineteenth century as the
result of Alexander's challenge to Persian hegemony, has resulted
in a tendency to understand Hellenistic culture as a syncretistic
homology. Although common systemic structures are indeed
identifiable as defining a Hellenistic culture,[2] we must take care not
to lose sight of such cultural differences as exist, for example,
between views of self-identity, within this system.

The emergence of individualism in the Hellenistic world did
not signal the promise of potential that characterized Renaissance
humanism but presented rather a problematic to be solved in
response to those transformations that characterized the
Hellenistic period. A locative image of the cosmos had been

This paper was read at the Fifteenth Congress of the International Association for
the History of Religions in Sydney, Australia, August 1985, under the title, "Identity
and Self-knowledge in the Syrian Thomas Tradition," and was published in *Identity
Issues and World Religions*, the Proceedings of the Congress, Victor C. Hayes, ed.
(Bedford Park, South Australia: AASR, 1986). It is reprinted here with minor revisions, by permission.

replaced by the exploded topography of what came to be termed the Ptolemaic system. The ascent of Alexander's Greco-Macedonian empire had challenged the traditional social conventions of political identity with its imposed but often unrealized cosmopolitan ideals. The collective piety of political allegiance or that of antiestablishment Dionysian *orgia* as portrayed in Euripides' *Bacchae* gave way to the labyrinthian wanderings of Apuleius's Lucius. And the classical speculations of Plato and Aristotle about a metaphysical and cosmological order of things were replaced by the ethical concerns of Hellenistic philosophy. These Hellenistic transformations all generated the question asked of Jesus by the anonymous everyman: "What must I do?" (Mark 10:17).

Stoic and Gnostic ethics represented alternative responses to the new exigencies of existence represented by the Hellenistic world. Both accepted *heimarmenē*, or a natural fate, as the normalizing principle of the cosmos, more than the power of any sovereign, whether emperor or god. And both knew the disastrous effects of the passions, of the sensuous world, for self-knowledge. Neither responded, however, in terms of fixed systems of thought; they represented, rather, antithetical strategies of existence within a contiguous cultural and historical context.

The Stoics applied traditional philosophical values to the new individualism and taught the taming of human passions by self-examination in order to effect a harmonious relation with the external order of things. True freedom was the moral freedom of a philosophical self-knowledge which recognized and conformed to an assumed orderly principle of the cosmos.

Gnostics, on the other hand, represented a Hellenistic strategy of individual existence par excellence. They were rarely, if ever, organized into autonomous institutional forms but articulated their perspective through existing religious and philosophical alternatives.[3] They repudiated this world, along with its ruling powers, altogether. This anticosmic rebellion was based upon their absolute certainty of a knowledge which they believed was revealed from beyond the normalizing cosmic limits of what, hitherto, had been considered possible.[4]

To the new exigencies of existence represented by the Hellenistic world, Gnostic thought responded, "Know yourself, and you will possess," in the well-known words of the second-century Valentinian Gnostic, Theodotus: "knowledge of who we were, and what we have become, where we were or where we were placed, whither we hasten, from what we are redeemed, what birth is and what rebirth" (*Exc. Thd.* 78.2).[5] Or, again, in the words of his contemporary, the Gnostic Christian theologian, Clement of Alexandria: "It is then . . . the greatest of all lessons to know one's self. For if one knows himself, he will know God" (*Paedagogus* 3.1).[6]

The Delphic maxim concerning self-knowledge was widely cited in Greek and Hellenistic literature generally,[7] and in Gnostic literature specifically.[8] Since the *Alcibiades I*, attributed to Plato, self-knowledge had been at the center of Western ethical thought. When the young Alcibiades wishes to begin his public life (123^d), Socrates intervenes and, with reference to the Delphic inscription, seeks to lead Alcibiades to a knowledge of himself (124^a–124^b), for, by knowing oneself, the political leader knows the proper affairs of others and thereby the affairs of state (133^d–134^a).

To Alcibiades' query about how he might achieve this self-knowledge (124^b), Socrates responds that he would come to know himself if he takes care of himself (*epimelēsthai sautou;* 127^c, 132^c). Thus, for the Western tradition, self-knowledge was the function of certain obligations associated with taking care of the self.[9] An Eastern "gnostic" tradition, probably centered in Edessa, presents Thomas, contrary to the Western canonical tradition of a "doubting" Thomas (John 20:24–29), as the exemplum of individual self-knowledge.[10] This tradition can be traced from the *Gospel of Thomas* through a *Book of Thomas*, both from the second codex of the Nag Hammadi library, to the *Acts of Thomas*.[11] The association of taking care of oneself with the Delphic maxim concerning self-knowledge, which was characteristic of Greco-Roman ethical literature since Plato, is characteristic of this Eastern Thomas tradition as well, but as an interdiction rather than an obligation.

The Syrian *Acts of Thomas*, dated in the early third century C.E.,[12] belongs to an Eastern collection of apocryphal *Acts of the Apostles* attributed, since the fifth century, to Leucius Charinus, a supposed companion of the apostle John.[13] The *Acts of Thomas* is generally considered to belong to a genre of Hellenistic-Oriental romances, a somewhat loosely defined genre of literature characterized primarily by the adventurous travels of a hero to exotic foreign places and by his erotic encounters.[14] This "romance" of Thomas elaborates earlier themes of the Thomas tradition in terms of the apostle's supposed missionary activities in India.

The *Acts of Thomas* begins with the disciples of Jesus conducting a lottery to determine which region of the world each would evangelize. Thomas draws India but, as a Hebrew, is reluctant to travel to so foreign a region. Jesus forces the issue by selling him as a slave to the Indian merchant Abban, who soon sets sail with Thomas in tow. They arrive first in Andrapolis during a citywide festival celebrating the marriage of the local king's only daughter.

During the celebrations, a cupbearer unexpectedly slaps Thomas, presumably because of the attention shown him by one of the entertainers, a Hebrew flute girl. Responding to this unwarranted attack, Thomas promises that "My God will forgive this injury in the world to come, but in this world he will show forth his wonders, and I shall even now see that hand that smote me dragged by dogs" (*AcTh.* 6)—a somewhat uncharitable response by canonical standards. And indeed, according to the Acts, when the cupbearer goes out to the well for water, he is slain and dismembered by a lion and a black dog picks up the right hand, which had struck Thomas, and carries it back to the party.

Having now attracted the attention not only of the flute girl but

of the entire gathering, Thomas is conscripted by the anxious
king to pray for the marriage of his daughter. After praying that
Jesus might do "the things that help and are useful and profitable"
for these newlyweds, Thomas blesses the couple and departs.

When everyone finally leaves, the bridegroom anxiously
approaches his bride but is amazed to find Jesus, in the likeness of
his twin, Thomas, chatting with his new wife in the bedroom. As
the three of them sit down together to discuss the situation, Jesus
counsels the newlyweds to abandon the "filthy intercourse" they
obviously had been anticipating and

> become holy temples, pure and free from afflictions and pains
> both manifest and hidden, and you will not be girt about with
> care for life [*phrontidas biou*] and children, the end of which is
> destruction. . . . But if you obey and keep your souls pure unto
> God, you shall have living children . . . and shall be without
> care [*amerimnoi*]. [*AcTh.* 12]

Unexpectedly for the modern reader, and likely for Thomas's
non-Christian contemporary as well, the bridegroom thanks Jesus
for this unsolicited but timely advice and for revealing his corrupt
and morally sick condition by directing him to seek himself and to
know (*gnōnai*) who he was and who and how he now is (*AcTh.*
15).

The *Acts of Thomas* presents a self-knowledge constituted by
secret teachings (*gnōsis*), which Thomas has received from Jesus
(*AcTh.* 39) and which are now recorded in this account of his
missionary activities. Contrary to the Western ethical tradition,
this self-knowledge results in a freedom from care (*aphrontis*,
amerimnos; AcTh. 12, 35). This antithetical relationship between
self-knowledge and taking care of oneself is soteriological. In her
rejection of "filthy intercourse" (see also *AcTh. 43*), the bride did
not become yoked to a "short-lived" husband but was wedded to
the "true man" (*AcTh.* 14); the bridegroom came to know his true

self (*AcTh.* 15; see also 43 and 144); and even the flute girl found soteriological rest (*anapausis*) as a result of these events.[15] Similarly, in the third act of Thomas, a young man who had been killed by a giant serpent but resuscitated through Thomas's intercession concludes that "I have become free from care [*phrontidos*] . . . from the care [*phrontidos*] of night, and I am at rest [*anapaen*] from the toil of day" (*AcTh.* 34).

In the Socratic obligation to take care of oneself, two points of view intersect, the political and the erotic. When the young Alcibiades wishes to enter political life, he submits to Socrates, the first of his lovers (*Alc. I* 103*ᵃ*, 104*ᵉ*). According to Socrates, to know oneself one must know both one's body, one's sexuality, and how to participate in the sociopolitical world. This positive relationship between techniques of self and that which is not self—teachers, the city (or the sociopolitical realm), and the cosmos—is a persistent theme of Western philosophizing.

Similarly, in the *Acts of Thomas*, a political context is established when Thomas attends the wedding celebration of the princess at the court of the king and then participates in this royal celebration by blessing the union. However, this participation in public life is required of Thomas against his will, whereas Alcibiades aspired to political life. An erotic context is also established in the *Acts of Thomas* when the groom approaches his new bride for the first time. However, the new wife submits not physically to her husband but spiritually to the "true man," Jesus.

Jesus shows the bride and groom, even as Socrates taught Alcibiades, that self-knowledge is not of the body but of the soul (*Alc. I* 130*ᵉ*, 132*ᵇ⁻ᶜ*). However—and here the two traditions diverge—in the Platonic and later Stoic traditions, self-knowledge requires practices of taking care of oneself characterized by a network of obligations and services, whereas in the Eastern Thomas tradition, self-knowledge results in a carefreeness characterized by a network of interdictions.

The Coptic *Book of Thomas*, from the same Nag Hammadi codex

as the *Gospel of Thomas*, is dated earlier in the second century C.E.
than the *Acts of Thomas*.[16] It introduces the same interdiction as
does the *Acts*, but in the context of a revelatory dialogue. This
form is revealed as pseudodialogical, however, when Thomas tells
Jesus that "It is you Lord whom it benefits to speak, and me to
listen" (*BkTh*. 142.9).

Although Jesus points out that the secret teachings are already
known to and have been pondered by Thomas, he invites Thomas
to examine himself in order to know who he is in light of this
revelation. Jesus does not consider it seemly that his twin brother
should be ignorant of himself (*BkTh*. 138.10–12): "For he who has
not known himself has known nothing, but he who has known
himself has at the same time already achieved knowledge about
the Depth of the All" (*BkTh*. 138.16–18).

The relation between self-knowledge and rejection of the world
is clearly summarized by Jesus in a concluding section of the *Book
of Thomas*.[17] Those who have not received the revealed doctrine
are ignorant and, thus, are renounced. Their soul has been
corrupted by the body and by the world. The blessed, on the
other hand, are those who, like Thomas, have prior knowledge of
these things.

The general rejection of the world by the *Book of Thomas*
(143.13f.) does not explicitly refer to political involvement as does
the *Acts of Thomas*, but it is explicit concerning rejection of the
body.[18] The body is transitory (*BkTh*. 139.4); it decays and
perishes (*BkTh*. 139.5). This cycle of fleshly life derives finally from
"intimacy with women and polluted intercourse" (*BkTh*. 144.9f.,
139.8–10), the fire of lust "that scorches the spirits of men" (*BkTh*.
140.3f.), "the bitter bond of lust for those visible things that will
decay and change" (*BkTh*. 140.33f.).

The rejection of world by Jesus is summarized in the *Book of
Thomas* by the interdiction against *prooush bios* (*BkTh*. 141.12–14,
38f.). The Coptic word *rooush* translates not only *phrontis* and
merimna, the words for "care" used in the Greek version of the

Acts of Thomas, but also *epimeleia*, the technical term for "care" in the Western ethical tradition.[19] This interdiction against any concern or care for this life seems to include the practice of care itself. When Thomas shows care (*merimna*) for those deprived of the kingdom (*BkTh.* 142.3–5), he is persuaded by the Savior not to care for them, for their deprivation is the lot of the ignorant (*BkTh.* 142.11–19).

The obligation to know oneself is central also to the teachings of the *Gospel of Thomas*. One of the first things Jesus tells his disciples in this *Gospel* is that "When you come to know yourselves, then you will become known, and you will realize that it is you who are the sons of the living Father. But if you will not know yourselves, you dwell in poverty and it is you who are that poverty" (*GosTh.* 3). Consequently, they are repeatedly exhorted to seek this knowledge until it is found (*GosTh.* 2, 92, 94). This is a difficult task, however, for the knowledge that is to be sought has already come, and the disciples have not recognized it (*GosTh.* 51). As Jesus says in another passage, "That which you have will save you if you bring it forth from yourselves" (*GosTh.* 70).

Dated from the second half of the first century c.e. to the first half of the second century c.e.,[20] the opening lines of the *Gospel of Thomas* differ significantly from the *Book of Thomas* only in that Thomas himself is represented as recording "the secret sayings which the living [or resurrected] Jesus spoke" (*GosTh.*, incip.), rather than the secretary, Mathias (*BkTh.* 138.1–3). Thomas, however, is not simply the secretary for Jesus and the other disciples in the *Gospel*, for Jesus takes him aside and reveals to him knowledge not shared with the other disciples (*GosTh.* 13). In other words, the knowledge that saves and is revealed by Jesus only to Thomas (*GosTh.* 13) is an inner knowledge (*GosTh.* 108), which Thomas has written down (*GosTh.*, incip.) for whoever has ears to hear (*GosTh.* 8, 21, 63, 65, 96) or, for his readers, eyes to see.

For the *Gospel of Thomas*, self-knowledge seems to result in a negative stance toward the external world: "Whoever finds himself is superior to the world" (*GosTh*. 111). However, this priority of knowledge to action is not so clear as it comes to be in the *Book of Thomas*. Other sayings of Jesus in the *Gospel* seem to suggest that self-knowledge is the result of certain practices of world rejection: "Be on your guard against the world," Jesus warns (*GosTh*. 21), for "If you do not fast as regards the world, you will not find the Kingdom" (*GosTh*. 27). In either case, the self-knowledge is clearly understood by the *Gospel of Thomas* to be inner, apart from, and other than the external world: "Whoever has come to understand the world has found [only] a corpse" (*GosTh*. 56).

Although a specific interdiction against care does not appear in the *Gospel of Thomas*, the earliest of the Thomas texts, its sense is clearly present. Like the *Acts of Thomas*, the *Gospel* rejects not only the external "world" generally but also the sexual and political activities of this world specifically. "Blessed is the womb which has not conceived and the breasts which have not given milk," Jesus tells an adoring woman (*GosTh*. 79), for only those who "make the male and the female one and the same, so that the male not be male nor the female female," will enter the Kingdom (*GosTh*. 22). And again Jesus commands his disciples: "Give Caesar what belongs to Caesar, give God what belongs to God, and give Me what is Mine" (*GosTh*. 100; see also 81, 110). Self-knowledge for the *Gospel of Thomas*, therefore, is other than the social relationships required by sexual and political activity. "Many are standing at the door," Jesus says, "but it is the solitary who will enter the bridal chamber" (*GosTh*. 75; see also 49).[21]

The rejection of sociopolitical obligations in the Eastern Thomas tradition stands in marked contrast to their necessary inclusion within practices of self-identity in the Western tradition. In the Platonic and later Stoic traditions, self-knowledge is the result of a "caring for the self," characterized by a network of external obligations and practices, whereas in the Thomas tradition self-knowledge is a revealed or prior knowledge, resulting in a carefreeness characterized by inner discipline within a network of interdictions. This revealed "prior" knowledge is the subject of the "gnostic" Thomas literature.

The Thomas tradition consists of the secret teachings of Jesus "received" by "listening" to the revelations of Jesus (*GosTh.*, incip.; *BkTh.* 138.1–4, 142.9f.; *AcTh.* 39),[22] which, according to the *Gospel of Thomas*, Thomas wrote down, whereas according to the *Book of Thomas* they were written down by a secretary. Whatever the historical origin of these pseudodialogues, they claim to reveal a prior *gnosis* in writing. They do not recommend dialogic activity, for which the questioning Thomas of the Western canon might have served as model, but instead record a particular content to be read and known. This self-emphasis by the Thomas tradition on the writing of revelation suggests a solitary, inner technique of reading the self.

The practice of reading as a technique for knowing self is described in the *Acts of Thomas* itself, in the "Hymn of the Pearl," which was sung by Thomas while in prison to encourage his fellow inmates (*AcTh.* 108–13). In this famous hymn, a king's son, the first-person author of the song, is sent forth to seek a precious pearl, an allegorical designation for his true self,[23] which is guarded by a ferocious serpent in Egypt. But the son soon forgets his task, and himself, as he takes up a foreign way of life.

The royal parents write their lost son a letter, identical to what is already "written" in his heart, recalling him to its contents so that he might know who he really is. When the son reads this letter, he is awakened to his true self and is able successfully to complete his quest for the pearl and return home.

In this hymn, the son's knowledge of himself is arrived at by reading a text. This text reveals a prior knowledge of his true self, already written within, but forgotten. In other words, this Eastern tradition represents a practice of reading the self in which the reader is disclosed to himself.

This technique of "reading of the self" recalls the thesis advanced by Richard Reitzenstein early in this century of a genre of *Lese-Mysteria*, or literary mysteries.[24] This genre, he argued, preserved the outward form of a Hellenistic mystery religion through a series of discursive and doctrinal writings. If the reader of such a literary mystery were one who had turned away from the world, the literary presentation would affect him just as if he had actually participated in a mystery ritual.[25] A.-J. Festugière has described the enigmatic Orphic literature as such a literary mystery,[26] following the lead of Pausanias, who equated a reading of Orphic writings with the witnessing of initiation at the Eleusinian Mysteries (1.37, 4).

Reinhold Merkelbach also has argued that the Hellenistic romances were written in the service of the Hellenistic mystery cults.[27] Though his view has been challenged,[28] it is generally agreed to hold true for two late romances, Apuleius's *Golden Ass* and the *Acts of Thomas*.[29] Apuleius's romance is clearly propaganda for the Hellenistic cult of Isis, whereas the *Acts of Thomas* presents a Christian-gnostic mystery of redemption.[30] As such, their point is not to recommend dialogic—or social—activity but, like the *Gospel* and the *Book of Thomas*, to present a particular content through the written word. The reading of such texts constituted a hermeneutics of the self.

In conclusion, two differently situated technologies of the Hellenistic self may be identified. The first, which is characteristic of the Western ethical tradition, might be termed an epistemological technology of self. This tradition emphasizes the activity of self-disclosure always in terms of an other. By disclosing oneself in dialogue, self was constituted. The second, exemplified by the Eastern Thomas tradition, might be termed an ontological technology of self. This tradition emphasizes the discernment or deciphering of what the self already is. This knowledge is reclaimed by passive listening and, later, through the solitary activity of reading. The first, dialogic activity, is social. The second, contemplative activity, was more conducive to the Syrian Encratitic technology of self generally considered to have been introduced to Western Christianity by John Cassian only at the end of the Hellenistic period in the early fourth century.[31]

Notes

1   Peter Brown, "The Rise and Function of the Holy Man in Late Antiquity" (1972), in *Society and the Holy in Late Antiquity* (Berkeley: University of California Press, 1982), p. 106.

2   Luther H. Martin, "Why Cecropian Minerva? Hellenistic Religious Syncretism as System," *Numen* 30 (1983): 131–45.

3   Kurt Rudolf, *Gnosis: The Nature and History of Gnosticism*, 2nd rev. ed., trans.; ed. Robert McLachlan Wilson (San Francisco: Harper and Row, 1983), pp.54–55.

4   The ascetic rejection of the ethical in its conventional sense suggests the basis for representing its Gnostic ethic as "licentious." Based upon accusations by Christian apologists, it has been argued, at least since the end of the nineteenth century, that the ascetic renunciation of the sensuous nature of the self had a counterpart in a libertine indifference toward the sensuous (Adolf Harnack, *History of Dogma* [1885], translated from 3rd German ed. by Neil Buchanan, 7 vols. [New York: Russell and Russell, 1958], 1:263), and even a "positive obligation" to violate this-worldly ethical standards (Hans Jonas, *The Gnostic Religion*, 2nd ed., rev. [Boston: Beacon Press, 1963], p. 273).

5   *The Excerpta ex Theodoto of Clement of Alexandria*, ed. and trans. Robert P. Casey (London: Christophers, 1934).

6   Trans. as *The Ante-Nicene Fathers*, ed. Alexander Roberts and James Donaldson, vol. 2 (Buffalo, N.Y.: Christian Literature Publishing House, 1885).

7   Eliza Gregory Wilkins, *"Know Thyself" in Greek and Latin Literature* (1917; rpt. Chicago: Ares, 1980), especially the compilation of passages in which the maxim is either explicitly cited or indirectly expressed (pp. 100–4).

8   Rudolf, *Gnosis*, p. 113; and Hans Dieter Betz, "The Delphic Maxim GNOTHI SAUTON in Hermetic Interpretation," *Harvard Theological Review* 63 (1970): 465–84.

9   Foucault, Chapter 2 herein, and *The History of Sexuality*, vol. 3, *The Care of the Self*, trans. Robert Hurley (New York: Pantheon, 1986), pp. 37–68. Wilkins, *Know Thyself*, pp. 60–61.

10   On the identity of the Eastern with the Western Thomas, see Helmut Koester, "GNOMAI DIAPHOROI: The Origin and Nature of Diversification in the

History of Early Christianity," in *Trajectories through Early Christianity*, ed. James M. Robinson and Helmut Koester (Philadelphia: Fortress Press, 1971), pp. 127–28, 133–34. On the origins of Christianity in Syria, see A. F. J. Klijn, *The Acts of Thomas*, supplement to Novum Testamentum V (Leiden: Brill, 1962), pp. 30–33; Arthur Voeoebus, *History of Asceticism in the Syrian Orient*, 2 vols. (Louvain: CSCO, 1958–60); and Han J. W. Drijvers, "Facts and Problems in Early Syriac-Speaking Christianity," *Second Century* 2 (1982):157–75.

11   Robinson and Koester, *Trajectories*, pp. 126–143; see also John D. Turner, *The Book of Thomas the Contender* (Missoula, Mont.: Scholars Press, 1975), pp. 233–39; and Drijvers, "Facts and Problems," pp. 157–75.

12   Syriac text, with English translation by W. Wright, in *Apocryphal Acts of the Apostles*, 2 vols. (London: Williams and Norgate, 1871); Greek text, in *Acta Apostolorum Apocrypha*, ed. R. A. Lipsius and M. Bonnet (1903; Darmstadt: Wissenschaftliche Buchgesellschaft, 1959); introduction and translation by Gunther Bornkamm, in *New Testament Apocrypha*, ed. E. Hennecke and W. Schneemelcher, trans. and ed. R. McL. Wilson, 2 vols. (Philadelphia: Westminster Press, 1965) 2:442–531.

13   Bornkamm, in *New Testament Apocrypha*, p. 427; W. Schneemelcher and K. Schaeferdiek, in *New Testament Apocrypha*, 2:178–88.

14   Albin Lesky, *A History of Greek Literature*, trans. James Willis and Cornelis de Heer (New York: Crowell, 1966), pp. 857–79; Ben Edwin Perry, *The Ancient Romances: A Literary-Historical Account of Their Origins* (Berkeley: University of California Press, 1967); and P. G. Walsh, *The Roman Novel: The "Satyricon" of Petronius and the "Metamorphoses" of Apuleius* (Cambridge: Cambridge University Press, 1970).

15   See *AcTh*. 142 where carefreeness (*aphrontis*) is equated with "rest."

16   *The Book of Thomas the Contender*, trans. John D. Turner, in James M. Robinson, gen. ed. *The Nag Hammadi Library* (San Francisco: Harper, 1977), pp. 188–94.

17   This section originally may have been a separate work (Turner, *The Book of Thomas the Contender* (1975), pp. 164–199, 215–25).

18   Ibid., p. 235.

19   W. E. Crum, *A Coptic Dictionary* (Oxford: Oxford University Press, 1939) p. 307*b*.

20   But see, e.g., Drijvers, "Facts and Problems," p. 173.

21   For "solitary" the Coptic text uses the Greek word *monachos* ("monk").

22   In the *Acts of Thomas*, the Greek word used for "receive" (*dechomai*) also means "to listen."

23   Richard Reitzenstein, *Hellenistic Mystery-Religions: Their Basic Ideas and*

Significance, 3rd ed. (1927), trans. John E. Steely (Pittsburgh: Pickwick Press, 1978), p. 58; Jonas, *Gnostic Religion*, pp. 125–26.

24 Reitzenstein, *Mystery-Religions*, pp. 51–52, 62.

25 Ibid., pp. 51–52.

26 A.-J. Festugière, *L'idéal religieux des grecs et l'évangile* (Paris: Lecoffre, 1932), and "Les mystères de Dionysos," *Revue biblique* 44 (1935): 192–211, 366–96.

27 Reinhold Merkelback, *Roman und Mysterium in der Antike* (Munich and Berlin: Beck, 1962).

28 E.g., Perry, *Ancient Romances*.

29 Helmut Koester, *Introduction to the New Testament*, vol 1, *History, Culture, and Religion of the Hellenistic Age*, trans. Helmut Koester (Philadelphia: Fortress Press, and Berlin and New York: Walter de Gruyter, 1982), p. 139.

30 Bornkamm, in *New Testament Apocrypha*, 2:429.

31 *Oxford Dictionary of the Christian Church*, ed. F. L. Cross (Oxford: Oxford University Press, 1958), p. 243. On Cassian, see Owen Chadwick, *John Cassian: A Study in Primitive Monasticism*, 2nd ed. (Cambridge: Cambridge University Press, 1968).

Four THEATERS OF HUMILITY AND

SUSPICION: DESERT SAINTS AND

NEW ENGLAND PURITANS

WILLIAM E. PADEN

If late classical monastic ideals represent one great prototype of Christian self-examination, puritanism represents another. Within the premise of our seminar, the two traditions are not simply antiquated Western ideologies but techniques and systems of behavior that form part of a history of subjectivity. A comparison of the self-subjection of monks and Puritans will sharpen the definition of these contrasting versions of the art of renunciation.

In many ways the two systems represent extreme poles of Christian spirituality. The monasticism of John Cassian, with its roots in Egyptian asceticism, embodies the classic pursuit of salvation or "purity of heart" through vigorous, systematic training. Puritanism, as the extreme form of Reformation Protestantism, is the last expression of a second religious trajectory: the way of "grace alone," based on the writings of Saint Paul, Saint Augustine, and Calvin, that proclaimed the human self utterly incapable of contributing to its own salvation. The Puritan movement inherited this myth and worked out its severest applications. The problem here was no longer "the world" but rather the self. Where the monk could differentiate soul from environment in a methodical way and subject the forces of sin and worldliness to his purity of will and achievement, the Puritan self found no such inner strength. An imposter, the self cannot by nature save itself. The self's own instrumentality is what is suspect.

This chapter focuses on examples of the contrastive aspects of the monastic and Puritan "self," including the ways that the two systems are governed by different polarities.

John Cassian's *Institutes* and *Conferences*,[1] written between 419 and 428, set the standards for Western monasticism and were influential throughout the Middle Ages. I will begin by outlining the system that appears to dominate Cassian's "path of the soul's perfection" and follow this with an examination of the Puritan suspicion of self, referring here especially—in honor of the regional setting of our seminar—to the example of the seventeenth-century New England divine, Thomas Shepard (1605–49)[2] and his *Journal*. The chapter concludes with comparisons and reflections that derive from the contrast.

John Cassian (c. 360–c. 434), perhaps of Scythian origin, lived many years in the monastic settings of the Egyptian desert before eventually settling in Marseilles and founding two large monasteries there. His writings conveyed the atmosphere and ideals of his Eastern mentors, whose spiritual prestige was then at its height.

For our purposes it is important to see that Cassian's path had a fixed goal and a specific method to achieve that goal and thus constituted a system whose component parts were unambiguously mapped out. The initial step, for Cassian, was renouncing the world. Such renunciation was the necessary condition for becoming a monk and marked off the initiate's goals from those of worldly professions. Abbots and holy men embodied living paradigms of the viability and successes of the path of purity. The monk knew what kind of behavior was to be avoided and what kind of behavior was to be fostered, and he knew the names of all the internal enemies. Cassian knew exactly why he had abandoned "our kinsfolk, our country, honours, riches, the delights of this world, and all kinds of pleasures," namely, to achieve purity of heart (*First Conf. of Abbot Moses* 4–5). His world was not a haphazard pilgrimage left to divine providence but a rigorous program of training in humility—the condition of entrance to the next world.

Cassian's system was clearly polarized. Within it, every act revealed godliness or its opposite. Through discretion and determination purity could be achieved and the forces of impurity uprooted and overthrown. The lines were clearly drawn. Such partitioning was crystallized by the fact that ungodliness could be labeled and objectivized. Most of Cassian's *Institutes* comprised a definition of the eight principal "faults" against which the monk should struggle: gluttony, lust, covetousness, anger, dejection, boredom, vanity, and pride. Cassian explained the causes and cures for each. Without the skills to combat them, the monk would become "subject" to these vices. Applying the skills, the vices would become subject to the monk's determination.

Cassian's vocabulary highlights the active, determinative character of this system. There is consistent use of terms for struggling, resisting, overcoming, fighting, prevailing. He relies on words for attaining, achieving, gaining, winning victory. His writings are saturated with the language of vigilance, discrimination, watching, weighing. Such a lexicon is possible only where there is a fixed discrimination of opposite realms.

The regimen of perfection proceeds systematically by building upon succeeding levels of self-discipline. For example, the monk must refrain from overeating because one cannot enter larger spiritual arenas of combat if already "smitten down in a struggle with the belly." Through fasting, recollection of past defeats, "sighing at one time with horror at sin, at another time inflamed with the desire of perfection and saintliness," one should bring the body into subjection in order to prepare for bringing the mind into subjection (*Inst.* 5.14–21). Cassian's argument runs:

For if a man is unable to check the unnecessary desires of the appetite how will he be able to extinguish the fire of carnal

lust? And if a man is not able to control passions, which are
openly manifest and are but small, how will he be able with
temperate discretion to fight against those which are secret,
and excite him, when none are there to see? And therefore
strength of mind is tested in separate impulses and in any sort
of passion. [*Inst.*5.20]

Cassian's attitude toward the sin of pride is instructive here.
Certainly he believed that man could attain nothing on his own
without God's grace; yet his acknowledgment that "all is given by
God" was not a theory deemphasizing human effort but itself an
act of piety. The sin of pride is the sin of self-sufficiency and trust
in one's own power. And yet pride is here "just" a sin, a vice,
and not, as with Saint Augustine and the Calvinists, identified with
human nature itself. Thus, Cassian can innocently note that pride
is particularly threatening to "those who are perfect" (*Inst.* 12.1).
Pride can be counteracted by its antithesis, humility.

And so God, the Creator and Healer of all, knowing that pride
is the cause and fountainhead of all evils, has been careful to
heal opposites with opposites, that those things which were
ruined by pride might be restored by humility. [*Inst.* 12.8]

With humility itself conceived as such an antidotal medicine,
humans are hardly powerless. The monk became an expert in
selflessness, and thoroughgoing obedience to the abbot was an
effective part of this process. Pride, the "beast" in the following
passage, can be joined and subdued in battle:

Wherefore the Christian athlete who strives lawfully in the
spiritual combat and desires to be crowned by the Lord, should
endeavour by every means to destroy this most fierce beast,
which is destructive of all virtues, knowing that as long as this
remains in his breast he not only will never be free from all

kinds of evils, but even if he seems to have any good qualities, will lose them by its malign influence. For no structure (so to speak) of virtue can possibly be raised in our soul unless first the foundations of true humility are laid in our heart, which being securely laid may be able to bear the weight of perfection and love upon them. [*Inst.* 12.32]

The final terms of this exhortation, that is, building up a structure of virtue on the foundation of humility, express well the methodical, technological character of Cassian's spiritual world.

Cassian advocated a confident, discriminatory examination of self. His focus was on how the soul—which in the following quotation is the implied actor and overseer—must steadily and carefully monitor its own contested realms:

We should then constantly search all the inner chambers of our hearts, and trace out the footsteps of whatever enters into them with the closest investigations lest haply some beast . . . passing through has furtively left the dangerous marks of his track, which will show to others the way of access into the secret recesses of the heart, owing to a carelessness about our thoughts. And so daily and hourly turning up the ground of our heart with the gospel plough, i.e. the constant recollection of the Lord's cross, we shall manage to stamp out or extirpate from our hearts the lairs of noxious beasts and the lurking places of poisonous serpents. [*First Conf. of Abbot Moses* 22]

But note that subjectivity as a problem has not fully emerged here. The one who stamps out the lairs of beasts and serpents, the observing self, is not yet really suspect. Cassian's is a presubjective world, still governed by the transpersonal, cosmic opposition of divinity versus worldliness.

The Puritans adopted quite a different paradigm of holiness. Owen Watkins writes that for them "the only thing a man contributed to his salvation was the sin from which he was redeemed." [3] The Puritan tradition of self-examination, from the mid-sixteenth to well into the eighteenth century, specialized in practices based on this belief. [4]

Saint Paul wrote that salvation "depends not upon man's will or exertion but upon God's mercy" (*Rom.* 9:16), and it became the Puritan technique not to emphasize performance of spiritual or ethical "works," including any form of self-purification, but rather to *expose* the sinfulness of self so that divine mercy could be acknowledged and honored. The presumptuous, unconverted self was confronted with the Word of God met through preaching, prayer, and Scripture reading as well as through the daily self-exposure of journal keeping. Because divine "election" meant precisely life lived under God's mercy, the practice of unmasking self-righteousness became identical with the practice of demonstrating or allowing the presence of that divine providence. Puritan "techniques" did not generate salvation by human effort but were occasions for witnessing to a relationship.

For the Puritan, then, the significant antithesis was not between God (or soul) and world but between God and self. As one divine put it:

> Man's fall was his turning from God to himself; and his regeneration consisteth in the turning of him from himself to God. . . . [Hence,] self-denial and the love of God are all [one]. . . . Understand this and you will understand what original and actual sin is, and what grace and duty are. . . . It is self that the Scripture principally speaks against. . . . The very name of Self and Own, should sound in the watchful Christian's ears as very terrible, wakening words, that are next to the names of sin and satan. [5]

In his *Puritan Origins of the American Self*, Sacvan Bercovitch epitomizes a series of Puritan allusions to this theme:

Polonius states a humanist commonplace when he speaks of being true to oneself. Calvin sets out the Reformed position when he requires us to "rid our selves of all selfe-trust," and his words resound throughout Puritan literature. "Not what Selfe will, but what the Lord will," thundered Thomas Hooker. The self is "the great snare," "the false Christ," a spider's "webbe [spun] out of our bowels," the very "figure or type of Hell." To "lay downe God-self," to root out "the Devil's poison and venome or infection or Self," was at once "to kill the old Adam" in us, to defeat the infernal "rebels against the commone good, all [of them] private respects of mens selves," and to strike a blow against "Antichrist, that is, the SELFE in all." [6]

If the Antichrist is the "self" in all, subjectivity here is no mere innocent bystander simply caught between the forces of heaven and worldliness but is itself the primary antagonist to God. "Why," wrote Shepard, "shall I seek the glory and good of myself who am the greatest enemy, worse than the Devil can be, against myself, which self ruins and blinds me?" (*Autobiography*, 45).

The Puritans replaced Catholic confession to a priest with the confessional diary, an account book of one's state of sin. In Shepard's *Journal*, in which it has been noted that "the suspicion of his own hypocrisy is a thread of fire," [7] entries like the following abound:

March 18. I saw if my mind acted it spun nothing but deceit and delusion, if my will and affections acted, nothing but dead works. Oh, how do I need Christ to live in me! Yet I saw if a man hath eyes and life he will not lean on another to lead him and carry him as when he wants both; so here. I saw the Lord made me live by faith by making me feel a want of both, to distrust myself and trust more unto the Lord. [*Journal*, 92]

Certainly the diary was not an occasion for just reviewing the day's events, exposing personal experiences, or indulging in a relaxed reverie. Puritan journals, in fact, were the opposite of personal. There is scarcely a sentence in Shepard's log that does not subsume individual experience into the matrix of divine activity. The "work" of the journal was precisely to effect this linkage of self with biblical standards of measurement. The result of this scrutiny: demonstration of the need for mercy, gratefulness and admiration for divine providence, intimate acquaintance with one's need for humility, and thus fittingness for the Christian pilgrimage. Every night symbolized death, so that at the end of every day the Puritan might go over his "accounts" accordingly, and if his journal sheets "should prove his winding-sheet, it had been all one: for, he could say his work was done; so that death could not surprise him." [8]

Shepard relentlessly attacked all forms of "spiritual" self-deception. He challenged his congregations and readers to distinguish between love of self and love of God, going to great lengths in enumerating typologies of false holiness and other "cunning" forms of self-justification (*Works*, 65–108). Salvation is not had through any form of "mere sincerity" or "good desires." True holiness is impossible when we are concerned only to save ourselves or when we love God "only because he is good to us" (*Journal*, 85). Thus, false holiness fears sin because it is self-condemning, whereas true holiness fears sin because it "dishonours Christ." "Content not yourselves with your bare reformation and amending your lives," writes Shepard, for "this is but to cross the debts in thine own book; it remaineth uncancelled in the creditor's book still" (*Works*, 54). "Many of you," he exhorts, "trust to Christ, as the apricot tree that leans against the wall, but it is fast rooted in the earth: so you lean upon Christ for salvation, but you are rooted in the world, rooted in your pride, rooted in your filthiness, still" (*Works*, 108). Sinners "use Christ as a dishclout to wipe them[selves] clean" (*Works*, 108). Selves thus "forge" faiths of their own but "perish by catching at their own catch, and hanging on their own fancy and shadow" (*Works*, 107). Subjectivity itself has become a trap.

One of the rituals of self-doubt took place during membership tests for admission to the church. Shepard recounts how a candidate was asked by elders, "Do you never find a heart that can't prize Christ but had rather walk after the way of your own heart?" One might surmise that the applicant would have passed the oral exam by answering that indeed he always prized Christ above all else. But the recorded, actual answer was more on the mark:

> Yes, I have seen it many a time but I have considered that was the way to ruin both me and mine after me. I have searched to see whether I loved God's company or no and I have found indeed my opposition against it. Yet I have found in some poor measure that God hath helped me to take delight in his will.[9]

E. S. Morgan, reviewing this example, notes that the "perfectly phrased" answer represented "faith in its proper imperfection, and one may be sure that the candidate was admitted."[10]

All Puritan practices were founded on the paradox that godliness and self-assurance are inversely related. "We cannot feel the Lord's power nor acknowledge it," Shepard writes, "without feeling the contrary power first" (*Journal*, 167). Doubt and humiliation become avenues of hope; losses become occasions for thankfulness; tragedies become signs of divine instruction. Shepard, whose "holy ambition" was to "rely on mercy" (*Journal*, 91), could state that "you that never felt yourselves as unable to believe as a dead man to raise himself, you have as yet no faith at all" (*Works*, 108). "The greater part of a Christian's grace," he notes in his *Journal*, "lies in mourning for the want of it" (198). We must "keep the wound always open" (*Works*, 67). McGiffert perceptively observes that Shepard's *Journal* shows a "subtle psychological transaction whereby anxiety is transmuted into assurance which is transmuted into anxiety, in Sisyphean sequence." [11]

The two arenas of piety just described reflect radically different systems of representing self. In the first, in John Cassian's, the subjectivization of world has not yet taken place. One might say that it has not been allowed to occur. The monk renounces any possibility of self, in favor of soul, at the outset of his career, and his life thereafter is a progressive realization of the power of this initial act. But in the Puritan model the center of "gravity" shifts. The enemy is now a more formidable competitor and threat to God: man's own self. Because the Puritan has not renounced his worldly self totally, as the monks had, it is not surprising that the Puritan's self becomes freighted with ambiguity and even placed on a par with Satan.

Cassian's world is represented in terms of a visible goal and the necessary techniques for producing that goal. Onto the renunciate's newly chosen monastic environment a map has been superimposed, not of the forsaken Carthage or Rome but of selflessness, its enemies, and its degrees of perfection. Cassian begins a summary of how a monk can "mount up toward perfection" by noting that according to Scripture the beginning of salvation and wisdom is the fear of the Lord. Yet note how he immediately goes on:

> From the fear of the Lord arises salutary compunction. From compunction of heart springs renunciation, i.e. nakedness and contempt of all possessions. From nakedness is begotten humility; from humility the mortification of desires. Through mortification of desires all faults are extirpated and decay. By driving out faults virtues shoot up and increase. By the budding of virtues purity of heart is gained. By purity of heart the perfection of apostolic love is acquired. [*Inst.* 4, 43]

In this logical and rational system even the Jobian "fear of the Lord" becomes something simply factored into the progressive structuring of a goal. But in the more desperate, uncertain world of a Shepard this would be incredible: Fear of God is not just an element of spiritual regimen but exactly what undermines all systems of selfhood. The Puritan's "regimen" was the daily assault upon self by scriptural Word.

"Sin" functions differently in the two worlds. For Cassian it is something to be eliminated because it is incompatible with humility and perfection. For the Puritan the foundation of religiousness lies in the act of acknowledging sin, exposing one's unholiness, holding the mirror to one's "filthiness and vileness." Cassian's writings warn that the contemplation of transgressions could be a hindrance to meditation since the very recollection of sins can contaminate the mind with their "foul stink" and "shut out the spiritual fragrance of goodness" (*Conf. of Abbot Pinufius* 9). He notes that "a man is sure to be suffocated by the pestilential smells of the sewer as long as he chooses to stand over it or to stir its filth" (*Conf. of Abbot Pinufius* 10). But the Puritan physician found good medicine in the preaching and imageries of self-abasement, self-abhorrence, self-execration. Where Cassian labored to make himself worthy to receive Christ within, the Puritan labored to make sure he was unworthy.

For Cassian, unlike for Shepard, sin is conceived as a possessive force that inflicts itself on the self from the outside. Thus, the Eight Vices are agencies that "assault" the monk. They "attack" him, "injure" him, "insinuate" themselves on him. "As the moth injures the garment," writes Cassian, quoting Scripture, "and the worm the wood, so dejection the heart of man" (*Inst.* 9.2). Of the sin of vanity he stresses that "the more thoroughly a man has shunned the whole world, so much the more keenly does it pursue him" (*Inst.* 11.6). In turn, the monk's task is to "repel," "guard against," or "overcome" these pursuing and cunning forces, forces that may ultimately be the agency of the devil. But

Thomas Shepard rarely spoke of sin as an objective pursuant that was seeking "entrance" into the chambers of his heart. He himself was the agency of all fault.

For Cassian, the monk has seized a certain self-determining power by the act of rejecting the world of society and its regime. Whereas salvation is theoretically and admittedly conditional upon divine grace, the individual is de facto the creator of his own progress. "It is to a great extent in our power," he writes, "to improve the character of our thoughts and to let either holy and spiritual thoughts or earthly ones grow up in our hearts" (*First Conf. of Abbot Moses* 17). But in puritanism, Christian otherworldliness and the temporal world reconvened, and the point where they connected, the human self, became threatening, suspect, profane. Subjectivity, with all its assertiveness and absence of self-consciousness, had to be scourged and had to be subjected to consciousness of itself. It had achieved no great acts of renouncing the world to give confidence in its selflessness, and the Puritan felt all the more ineluctably dependent on God's power and honor.

The Puritan journal shows what happens to confession of sin in the absence of a Catholic confessor. The Protestant self here must in some way become both accused and accuser. With no earthly superior in the picture, the external, two-part dialectic of confessing and examining becomes an entirely internalized dialogue. Since for Protestants grace was based not in church sacramentalism but in direct faith in the Word of God, it followed that exposure of one's status as a sinner would be exhibited not in the public ritual arenas of *exomologesis*[12] but in the alchemical retort of the individual's own self-contradictoriness.

Cassian and the Puritan did have something in common. Within the typologies of Max Weber, they both represented the techniques of asceticism—"world-rejecting" and "innerworldly" subtypes, to be sure—rather than mysticism.[13] If the mystic is the one for whom the path to God is through the cessation of human activity or "work," the ascetic is the one for whom salvation involves precisely an active struggle, an attempt to transform self and to certify divine favor through rigor of conduct. And yet, as Weber notes,

> From the standpoint of a contemplative mystic, the ascetic appears, by virtue of his transcendental self-maceration and struggles and especially by virtue of his ascetically rationalized conduct within the world, to be forever involved in all the burdens of created things, confronting insoluble tensions. . . . The ascetic is therefore regarded as permanently alienated from unity with god, and as forced into contradictions and compromises that are alien to salvation.[14]

Cassian had been exposed to contemplative mysticism through his teacher, Evagrius. But whereas Evagrius had taught the techniques of stripping the mind of all contents to the point of complete self-forgetfulness, Cassian evidently believed that the "empty mind" might be demonic.[15] Both Cassian and Shepard had their contemplative moods, yet their practices led not to the classic mystical goal of self-abandonment but rather to the unceasing pursuit—albeit in their different ways—of self-reformation. Chadwick notes:

> Between Cassian and his younger contemporary and neighbour, St. Vincent of Lérins, there is a contrast. To express the sum of the monastic life, Vincent used the verse of the psalms, "Be still then, and know that I am God." Cassian practised a constant meditation upon Scripture, and was always quoting its texts. Yet this quotation does not occur in his works.[16]

Nor is it apt to be found in Puritan diaries. No such confidence, no such cessation of self, no such empty mind could be trusted.

McGiffert rightly senses the importance of examining closely

the use of the first-person pronoun in Shepard's *Journal*. He finds
there two facets of self, the observer and the observed, and his
analysis merits full citation:

> Day after day these pages declared their author's existence both
> as the self that suffers and as the self that observes, weighs, and
> tries to understand. Shepard's piety is above all else percipient.
> Metaphors of light and enlightenment pervade the *Journal*. "I
> saw" is his characteristic statement: "I saw how I was without
> all sense as well as sight of God, estranged from the life of God
> ..."; "... on Sabbath morning I saw the Lord frowning on me
> in several providences...."; "I saw the Lord had let me see my
> unbelief and desire the removal of it." Shepard sees, and is
> seen—a Chillingworth, as it were, and equally a Dimmesdale:
> there lies Shepard flattened out in wholly genuine anguish, but
> there, simultaneously, is that other Shepard, perpendicular,
> cognitively masterful, the seeing I, lifting his pen to make a
> diagnostic or prescriptive note in his *Journal*. There is
> something somehow god-like about the second Shepard—
> something that verges perilously near the abominable sins of
> presumption and pride. Could the "I" that so clamantly asserts
> itself lose itself? And if it could not be lost, how could it be
> saved? The difficulty, unrecognized but perhaps not unfelt, lay
> at the core of the piety that inscribed journals like Shepard's.
> The way the journal was kept, responsive to the needs that
> inspired its keeping, tended to cancel, in point of assurance and
> emotional aplomb, the value of keeping a journal at all.[17]

McGiffert's point provocatively opens up wider ranges of
questions. Shepard's spectator "I" may anticipate the percipient
self of Romantic and modern times, a self alternately inflated and
depressed by the disappearance of divinity. It may correspond to
the suspicious and cognitive self that indefinitely looks over
its own shoulder and observes its own observing, its own

fabrications. Certainly Puritan writing, in spite of its God-centered theology, not only presupposed the importance of self, the "seeing I," but also prefigured the modern division of self into opposing parts. Puritan consciousness was saturated with "I-ness" and implicit self-righteousness, and one may suspect that its self-deprecation was the inevitable shadow of its own self-assertion.[18] The paradoxical nature of the Puritan self was perhaps an inevitable consequence of its nonmonastic, noncelibate, worldly setting.

Puritan suspicion of self represented a practice with implications that go well beyond the mythological agenda that invented it. By the logic of reflexive self-examination, every religious assertion—including every act of confession and every act of self-accusation—could become suspect of its own possible self-deception. One cannot resist thinking here of analogies with Zen Buddhist dialectics that feature the abolition or "emptiness" of all entrapping subject–object schemas. Ultimately, the observing or accusing self must itself become subject to scrutiny and judgment of the most radical kind. Where the self is enlarged, as it was for the Puritans, to include both accuser and accused, it is a short step for the accuser to its own gallows.

Notes

1   All citations to Cassian's works are from *The Works of John Cassian*, trans. Edgar C. S. Gibson, in *Nicene and Post-Nicene Fathers*, ed. P. Schaff and H. Wace, vol. 11 (New York: Christian Literature Company, 1894).

2   Shepard was a first-generation minister in the colony of Massachusetts Bay, and along with John Cotton and Thomas Hooker is considered one of the exemplary early American Puritans. He came to the New World in 1635. Citations in text refer to his *Journal* (1640–42) and *Autobiography* (1646), as available in *God's Plot: The Paradoxes of Puritan Piety*, ed. Michael McGiffert (Amherst: University of Massachusetts Press, 1972). In addition, the text will draw from *The Works of Thomas Shepard*, 3 vols. (New York: AMS Press, 1967), a comprehensive collection of Shepard's sermons and other writings; hereafter referred to in the text as *Works*. All citations are from vol. 1.

3   Owen Watkins, *The Puritan Experience: Studies in Spiritual Autobiography* (New York: Schocken Books, 1972), p. 5.

4   An excellent study is Charles E. Hambrick-Stowe, *The Practice of Piety: Puritan Devotional Disciplines in Seventeenth-Century New England* (Chapel Hill: University of North Carolina Press, 1982).

5   Richard Baxter, cited in Sacvan Bercovitch, *The Puritan Origins of the American Self* (New Haven: Yale University Press, 1975), p. 17.

6   Bercovitch, *Puritan Origins*, p. 18.

7   McGiffert, Introduction, *God's Plot*, p. 17.

8   The Puritan James Janeway, cited in Watkins, *Puritan Experience*, pp. 20–21.

9   This episode is cited in Edmund S. Morgan, *Visible Saints: The History of a Puritan Idea* (New York: New York University Press, 1963), p. 91.

10   Ibid., p. 91.

11   McGiffert, *God's Plot*, p. 25.

12   See Foucault, Chapter 2, herein.

13   See Max Weber, *The Sociology of Religion*, trans. Ephraim Fischoff (Boston: Beacon Press, 1967). The chapter, "Asceticism, Mysticism, and Salvation Religion," pp. 166–83, is especially instructive on the contrast between asceticism and mysticism.

14   Ibid., p. 171.

15   Owen Chadwick, *John Cassian*, 2nd ed. (Cambridge: Cambridge University Press, 1968), p. 104.

16   Ibid., pp. 94–95.

17   McGiffert, *God's Plot*, pp. 18–19.

18   Bercovitch discusses this point (*Puritan Origins*, pp. 18–25).

Five HAMLET'S "GLASS OF FASHION":

POWER, SELF, AND THE REFORMATION

KENNETH S. ROTHWELL

> Reverence the sovereign power over things in the Universe; that is what
> uses all and marshals all. In like manner too reverence the sovereign power
> in yourself; and this is of one kind with that. For in you also this is what
> uses the rest, and your manner of living is governed by this.
> MARCUS AURELIUS, *Meditations* 5.21

In William Shakespeare's *Hamlet*, the medieval conflict between
body and soul turns into the modern tension between power and
self. Just as Michel Foucault in *The Order of Things* exemplifies the
intricacies of classical representation with a painting, Velasquez's
Las Meninas, so it is possible here to understand *Hamlet* as an
emblem for the quandaries and dilemmas that beset the history of
technologies of self. Whereas Foucault in *The Order of Things* was
concerned with the tensions of representation, the ways in
which signs and signified have encoded certainties and
uncertainties, Prince Hamlet at Elsinore draws attention to the
systems of coercion and persuasion, of enfranchisement and
disenfranchisement, that at once circumscribe and liberate him.
In *Hamlet* Shakespeare writes a history of the present that
dramatizes how self divorced from power remains unrealized.
Notwithstanding that he is already, as Ophelia says, the "glass of
fashion," [1] Prince Hamlet must refashion himself in the mold of
new technologies. [2]

Among many other things, *Hamlet* mirrors the dislocation
between power and self that was an offshoot of the Protestant
Reformation. When Martin Luther nailed his Ninety-five Theses

to the door of Wittenberg's Castle Church at noon on October 31, 1517, he did more than sever a political bond with Rome; he established a technology, or antitechnology, for underwriting the ordeal of the individual self. That ordeal can be identified as an anguished quest to relocate the power of unimpeachable authority within impeachable self. It was a movement from the God-centered discourse of theology and confession to the man-centered discourse of Freud and Jung. The usurpation of ecclesiastical by temporal power only created a fresh need for the reallocation and redistribution of power.

Indeed, when Henry VIII argued that the bishop of Rome had himself usurped the imperial power, the quarrel took on convolutions of virtually impossible complexity. From Christopher Marlowe's Dr. Faustus to Dostoevski's Raskolnikov, the dilemma of the impeachable self, the embryo for the alienated self, has colored art and life in ways unthinkable prior to the Reformation. At stake has been nothing less than the power to speak, define, and promulgate knowledge. The loss of the absolute truth leads first to equivocation and then to anarchy. The Reformation disenfranchisement of established truths, disruption of the mechanics of a civilization, subversion of normative values, underwrote the apocalyptic visions of the times: Pascal's "The eternal silence of these infinite spaces terrifies me"; Donne's "all coherence gone"; and of course Hamlet's "The time is out of joint—O cursed spite, / That ever I was born to set it right!" (1.5.188).

In ways perhaps forever lost to us, *Hamlet* seems to have been an artifact in the intellectual ferment of its times, so much so, as the title page of the 1603 quarto edition informs us, that it was especially played for the young men of Oxford and Cambridge universities. Putting aside for the moment its manifest and frequently observed allusions to Wittenberg,[3] that hotbed of Lutheranism, there is, for example, a way of allegorizing the play as code for the Reformation itself. In such a model "that

adulterate, that incestuous beast," the uncle Claudius, stands for
the usurping pope or monarch (depending on one's theological
orientation), who was tirelessly excoriated in the polemical tracts
as the very embodiment of the Antichrist.[4] Hamlet's ordeal rests
not only on fratricide and incest but on an outright violation of
the feudal bond. The royal bed of Denmark, that "couch for
luxury and damned incest," adumbrates the larger violation of
Denmark in general. Elsinore has witnessed a quantum leap from
the tolerable but authoritarian juridicial model of contract-
oppression to the intolerable and totalitarian arrangement of
domination-oppression.[5] Claudius's politic manner may conceal
this fact from others at the court but not from the penetrating
gaze of his nephew. How ironic that Rosencrantz, of all people,
should be allowed to utter the words "The cess of majesty / Dies
not alone" (3.3.15) when Hamlet himself should "cleave the
general ear" with tales of his father's victimization.

The subversion of the Roman hegemony by northern states, or
the subjugation of northern nations by Rome, as the case may be,
whether involving Luther, Calvin, Servetus, Zwingli,
Melanchthon, or Henry VIII, released primordial energies as
dangerous to the macrocosm of Europe as to the microcosm of
Elsinore. Throughout northern Europe the new indifference to
the legitimacy of traditional authority, the willingness to embrace
illegitimacy for a higher good, enmeshed nation after nation. And
efforts of usurper to legitimize the illegitimate increased in direct
ratio to the blatancy of the takeover. By comparison with the
reformers, even a Henry Bolingbroke, a Plantagenet by birth, had
a greater claim to being one of "God's anointed deputies" on
earth. To return to *Hamlet* as allegory for this historical
movement, Hamlet himself becomes the people of England, torn
between subservience to venerable and powerful institutions and
an emerging sense of self, and ever fearful, like Othello, that
"Chaos [may] come again" (*Oth.* 3.3.92).

In these broad terms, then, one can allegorize *Hamlet* as a dark conceit shadowing forth the Reformation. None of these hermeneutics would be in the slightest compelling, however, were it not for a text and subtext in the play itself that hints again and again at sensitivity to, or even awareness of, the religious ferment of the times. As a man of his own age, as well as all ages, Shakespeare could not easily have shut out the continuing dialogue over religious matters. For now, however, I would like to confine myself to three ways that *Hamlet* reflects the history of the Reformation mentality: (1) the portrait of Prince Hamlet as a student dissident awash in the riptides of Renaissance and Reformation discourse; (2) the testimony of the soliloquies to conflict between power and self; and (3) the abrupt change, indeed metamorphosis, in the character of Hamlet, akin to a regeneration of self, that takes place in the fifth act.

First, some of the obvious bric-a-brac from the reformist camp. Why, for example, the heavy-handed name dropping about "Wittenberg," which puts a frame around the first soliloquy? As the doctrinal seat of Lutheranism, the voice of Wittenberg sounded far and wide, arousing admiration in dissidents and loathing in the faithful. Claudius, the classic usurper struggling to legitimize illegitimacy, was particularly vulnerable to these heresies, of which rebellion against tyrants was one result.[6] He could therefore be especially concerned about the return of his unpredictable and moody stepson to a place of such notoriously rampant sedition: "For your intent / In going back to school in Wittenberg, / It is most retrograde to our desire" (1.2.112). The queen, Gertrude, echoes the king, though perhaps for less weighty motives: "I pray thee stay with us, go not to Wittenberg" (1.2.119). Immediately following the subsequent soliloquy ("O that this too too sallied flesh would melt" [1.2.129ff.]), Hamlet twice asks Horatio about Wittenberg: "And what make you from Wittenberg" (1.2.164); and "But what, in faith, make you from Wittenberg?" (1.2.168). Hamlet's eagerness, his insistence, suggests Wittenberg's attraction to him, as though it possessed some power, spiritual or intellectual, lost at Elsinore. Wittenberg seems some kind of Eden, an unfallen world, a forest of Arden, in contrast with the rottenness of Denmark, which is "a prison" at best.

The "student prince," as S. F. Johnson aptly named him,[7] it could be argued, has even been touched by the teachings of Philipp Melanchthon at Wittenberg, who in praise of astronomy linked the study of nature with praise of the Creator:

> To recognize God the Creator from the order of the heavenly motions and of His entire work, *that* is true and useful divination. . . . In the sky, God has represented the likeness of certain things in the church.[8]

Hamlet's own musings about "this majestical roof fretted with golden fire, why, it appeareth nothing to me" (2.2.301–2) suggest either a profound skepticism akin to Montaigne's Pyrrhonian suspense of judgment, or even covert nonbelief. Hamlet's sophomoric verse epistle to Ophelia, "Doubt thou the stars are fire, / Doubt that the sun doth move" (2.2.116ff.), though often read as supportive of the old Ptolemaic world view, may echo the theories about Copernicus at Wittenberg. In the late sixteenth century, Caspar Peucer, Melanchthon's son-in-law and disciple, was actually lecturing there on this and other recondite topics.[9]

That zeal for the "Philippists" at Wittenberg and the new vision of truth that they stood for also coincides with Hamlet's own positions against other forms of power. His "inky cloak" and "suits of solemn black" have quite rightly been attributed to melancholy chic, of the variety flaunted in a contemporary portrait of John Donne. As well, however, the costume accords with puritanical taste, perhaps that of a Zeal-of-the-Land Busy in Jonson's *Bartholomew Fair*, who was glad to "prophesy the destruction of fairs and May-games, wakes and whitsun-ales, and doth sigh and groan for the reformation of these abuses" (*BF*

4.6.91). If this comparison with Busy seems misplaced, then Petruchio and Malvolio may better serve to reveal attitudes not entirely dissimilar from Hamlet's: the former with his suspicion of outward show ("For 'tis the mind that makes the body rich," he tells Kate [*Shr.* 4.3.172]); and Malvolio with his horror of fleshly pleasures ("You must amend your drunkenness," he admonishes Sir Toby [*TN* 2.5.73]). Ascetic tendencies such as these contain their own ideological codes. For example, Hamlet, as well as sharing Petruchio's disdain for external finery, also shares Malvolio's contempt for drunkards. When Hamlet and Horatio overhear the "heavy-headed revel" of Claudius's ritual carousing (1.4.17), Hamlet warns his school friend that he may be forced to "drink deep" in conformity to the deplorable social customs at Elsinore.

A case also can be made that Hamlet's apparent misogyny stems as much from a Pauline understanding of women as from any "psychological" quirk. Hamlet knows full well the meaning of the "expense of spirit in a waste of shame" (Sonnet 129), as his nausea for Ophelia shows: "You jig and amble, and you [lisp], you nickname God's creatures and make your wantonness [your] ignorance" (3.1.144–46); or his disgust with Gertrude's middle-aged concupiscence: "Let the bloat king tempt you again to bed, / Pinch wanton on your cheek, call you his mouse, / And let him, for a pair of reechy kisses, / Or paddling in your neck" (3.4.182–85). Paul's words come to mind: "It is good for man not to touch a woman" (1 Cor. 7:1); or again, the famous utterance, "But if they cannot contain, let them marry: for it is better to marry than to burn" (1 Cor. 7:9). As is well known, the Protestant reformers reacted against what they took to be Roman abuse of the Gospels by searching for the primitive church in the writings of Saint Paul Whatever their other differences, Hamlet might have agreed with Laertes' distaste for a "churlish priest."

Hamlet's denial of the flesh and putative aversion to the attractions of the opposite sex imply a view of self different from that of established ecclesiastical and temporal power. Fear of usurpation of spirit by feminine wiles underlies his loathing for Ophelia. The word "spirit," as Shakespeare's Sonnet 129 shows ("Th'expense of spirit in a waste of shame"), carries both carnal and spiritual overtones. Hamlet's denial of the flesh emulates Christian asceticism. He rejects Ophelia, however, not only to serve God but to refashion himself. It is only through resisting the powerful orbit of court society that he can locate a greater power within himself. And the soliloquies in the first part of the play, which only partly disclose the inner turmoil, offer glimpses of Hamlet's anguish as he struggles to resolve self within the constraints of the power struggle in the hegemony of Denmark.

In truth, Hamlet's meditations reveal less about him than one might think. They are soliloquies, fictions of privacy in reality delivered under the surveillance of a huge audience at the public playhouse.[10] Contrivances of drama, they eschew the total revelation of innermost secrets characteristic of later discourses of interiority. Hamlet stops short of exposing "the secrets of his heart at the foot of the Throne," as called for in *The Confessions of Jean-Jacques Rousseau.*[11] In the soliloquies, the prince generally directs his thoughts outwardly toward Elsinore and his relationship with the court, not inwardly, as has often been thought, toward profound examination of self. What emerges is a psychodrama of selving filled with self-reproach for inaction, but very little scrutiny of deeper, hidden motives. He plays the sociologist in acknowledging Elsinore as a fallen world, "an unweeded garden / That grows to seed" (1.2.135–36); and, as Harold Jenkins has helpfully pointed out, identifies with the Hyperion figure of his father as opposed to the Satyr figure of Claudius.[12]

A more searching self-examination occurs in "O, what a rogue and peasant slave am I!" (2.2.550), after the affirmations of fidelity to the father's spirit of "I doubt some foul play" (1.2.255) and "thy commandement all alone shall live" (1.5.102). The pivotal event of this soliloquy is the abrupt shift from belief to doubt about the ghost's reliability. On the parapets, once past his formulaic greeting of the ghost, there was no hint of Hamlet's skepticism, and the ghost's remark, "I find thee apt," suggests the prince was indeed a star pupil. Now suddenly, after berating his own inaction as compared to the action of a mere player, Hamlet asks the stinging question, "Am I a coward?" (2.2.571). But at this moment of truth he veers away from examination of self to design the "mouse trap" for exposing Claudius's guilt: "The spirit that I have seen / May be a [dev'l], and the [dev'l] hath power / T' assume a pleasing shape" (2.2.598–600). Instead of uncovering the reasons for inactivity he covers up his own motive for delay. Somehow lacking is a moral authority for action, a bond between power and self, in order to proceed with plain duty. Hamlet's search for a motive to act is also the search for power to replace powerlessness. Hamlet's "Renaissance" side has prepared him better for the technologies of politics than his "Reformation" side has equipped him with a technology of self.

The more personal meditations in the "To be or not to be" soliloquy move away from Renaissance concern with political reality to Reformation topics, specifically the Protestantism of the "irenic" wing of French thinkers.[13] The words "to be or not to be,"[14] whether rooted in the Aristotelian sense of *esse* or taken to mean "to live or to die" or "to act or not to act" or "to avenge or not to avenge," indubitably define Hamlet's central dilemma. His inconsistencies and self-contradictions, doubts and fears, uncertainties and certainties, as he balances between the fallen world of Elsinore and the unfallen world of his dreams, emerge in the discourse of neo-Stoicism. In it, "fortune" sometimes interfaces with "predestination," or even "election," though I defer to Walter King's astute differentiation between "fate" and "providence."[15] Note, for example, how the pagan concepts of "fortune" and "philosophy" in this passage from Marcus Aurelius approximate Christian doctrines such as "providence" and "God," though the teleology in each instance is radically different.

Of man's life, his time is a point, his existence a flux, his
sensation clouded, his entire body's entire composition
corruptible, his vital spirit an eddy of breath, his fortune hard
to predict, his fame uncertain. . . . What then can be his escort
through life? One thing and one thing only, Philosophy.[16]

This separation between power and self, which Marcus Aurelius
saw as sometimes indicative of a malaise of soul,[17] continues in
successive soliloquies as Hamlet on the one hand speaks of
drinking "hot blood" and on the other hand of avoiding a
Nero-like stance in approaching Gertrude (3.2.390); saves
Claudius for a more "horrid hent" (3.3.88), even as the sword of
justice is raised in retribution; and wonders out loud if he is
indeed guilty of "some craven scruple" (4.4.40) as he observes
Fortinbras "find quarrel in a straw / When honor's at the stake"
(4.4.55–56).

A talisman of Hamlet's disorientation lies in the existence of not
one but at least two Hamlets.[18] The first of these personalities can
be identified with the myth of the Renaissance man, a centrifugally
oriented human being equipped with the techniques for reshaping
the world around him; the second, with the type of the reformer,
a centripetally directed person open to techniques for discovery
of the inner self. Renaissance man, one might say, courted
damnation; Reformation man craved salvation. In actuality,
of course, the technologies of self implicated with both the
Renaissance and the Reformation were often symbiotic,
but their presence in a single person invited explosive
contradictions.

In his perturbation over the state of the world, the first Hamlet
emerges as alienated from virtually everyone in power at Elsinore.
Hamlet in his feigned madness even acts out the prime role for
madness assigned by Foucault to conceal "beneath error the secret
enterprise of truth." [19] With Gertrude, the prince is rude; with
Claudius, snappish; with Polonious, impudent; with Laertes,

distant; with Ophelia, sardonic; with Rosencrantz and Guildenstern, condescending. Hamlet, symbolically garbed in his "customary suits of solemn black," is a figure so immune to routine social compromises that only Horatio and a ghost qualify for close companionship. The restlessness, the turmoil, the perturbation, the "antic disposition," the madness, the frenzy, the railing, the jesting, the meddling, the hectoring and sermonizing, the dread, the sarcasm, the wordplay, the bantering and punning, and the plain confusion of this mercurial character yield, however, at last to quite a different hero; one might even say an "antihero." This man of "wild and whirling words," as Horatio describes him (1.5.133), by the second scene of act 5 can serenely say, "There's a divinity that shapes our ends, / Rough-hew them how we will" (5.2.10–11).

Hamlet undergoes a profound shift not only in perception but also in behavior. This is not a Prince Hal removing a mask to reveal an inner self already in place; it is rather a Duke Frederick of *As You Like It*, who has become a "convertite." Written at about the same time as *Hamlet*, *As You Like It* shows that the phenomenon of conversion— or perhaps more accurately in Protestant terms of "regeneration"—was again on Shakespeare's mind, as indeed it was earlier when Kate Minola underwent an experience akin to Saint Paul's on the road to Damascus. On the road to Padua, Kate suddenly saw the "sun" as "moon" and the "moon" as "sun" (4.5.20). Hamlet has not so much "fashioned" himself as refashioned himself. A prince of Denmark by nature is entitled to a certain exemption from nurture.

Hamlet cannot know, of course, indeed does not seem terribly aware of the counterplot against him by Claudius and Laertes; or, perhaps he *knows* but in some transcendental way open only to saints and fools. The acceptance of a providential design, a universe no longer existentially "weary, stale, flat, and unprofitable" but essentially filled with meaning, surfaces in this fresh vision: "Not a whit, we defy augury. There is special providence in the fall of a sparrow. If it be [now], 'tis not to come; if it be not to come, it will be now; if it be not now, yet it [will] come—the readiness is all" (5.2.219–22). This prophetic speech, I take it, is not isolated, out-of-context pleading by a single character, such as Gloucester's belief in *King Lear* that we are "As flies to wanton boys" (4.1.36), but deeply embedded in the design. Hamlet's inward purgation has been accomplished at the price of his outward reputation; to realign power within himself he has had to surrender that power to someone else.

Perhaps I should put the matter another way: The avenger who has berated himself for inability to act ("Am I a coward?") accepts the role of antagonist instead of protagonist. He has fallen to rise, as it were. This metamorphosis in character—in some kind of Freudian slip Shakespeare even makes Hamlet years older in the graveyard scene—is one of the major mysteries of *Hamlet*. Presumably it does not spring from artistic failure, an inability of the playwright to impose consistency on his hero; rather, it is deliberate, planned, purposeful, artistically defensible.[20]

Usually thought of as caught between medievalism and modern times, Hamlet's dilemmas also grow out of the technologies of the converging and diverging currents of Renaissance and Reformation ideologies. That framework may offer a key to understanding the contradictions between the earlier and later Hamlet: a would-be man of action turned contemplative, a protagonist turned antagonist, or even—at the risk of egregious oversimplification— the man of the Renaissance turned man of the Reformation.

Hamlet's reformist tendencies often parallel the discourse of a French Protestant, Philippe Duplessis-Mornay (1549–1623). Duplessis, well known to such celebrated personages as Sir Philip Sidney and Michel de Montaigne, was the author, among many other tracts, of *Excellens traitez et discours de la vie et la mort* (Lausanne, 1576). There is also a body of circumstantial evidence connecting Shakespeare with Duplessis, the Sidney family, and

the Huguenot exiles in London.[21] Of primary interest here is the
ideology of Duplessis and the French reformers, which might
account for Hamlet's shift from perturbation to serenity, a shift
that parallels in many ways the "irenicist" attitudes that made the
French reformers the most tolerant of the dissenters.[22]

Duplessis's Huguenot writings, often revealing affinities of an
intertextual nature to *Hamlet*,[23] were peculiarly well equipped to
offer a paradigm for a new technology of self fashioned in neo-
Stoic and reformist ideologies. The followers of King Henry of
Navarre, the French king who led the Huguenots against the
Roman Catholics and then later sold them out (Paris was "worth a
mass"), brought a measure of tolerance and fellowship to religious
matters rare for the times. Protestantism had a very early history
in France even antedating Luther's ninety-five Theses; it had
always, however, been handicapped by a separate agreement
between pope and king to allow monarchical control over the
church. Hence, there was neither economic nor political profit in
supporting the Protestants, as was the case in Germany and
England. Perhaps out of the necessity of steering between the
peasants who remained loyal to Rome and the crown that had
made a covenant with Rome, the Huguenots learned to express a
commendable tolerance for persons of different beliefs. Thus the
chancelier l'hôpital in pleading to the States General at Blois in
1560 spoke of "the arms of charity, prayer, persuasion, and the
words of God. . . . Let us drop the wicked names of [our] factions.
Let us content ourselves with the title of Christians."[24] That
attitude embodies the spirit of irenicism implicit in the work of
Duplessis. The idea was not so much, as with Fortinbras, to find
quarrel in a straw as to transcend earthly quarrels with faith in a
divine providence.

Although Hebraism won out over Hellenism in the struggle for
ideological supremacy among the reformers, the Calvinists were
more likely than the Lutherans to lean on classical precedents.
Therefore the *prisci theologi*, pagans with prophetic powers such as

Marcus Aurelius and Seneca, figure especially heavily in the tracts of Duplessis. Throughout his canon is a sense of coming to terms with woe and turmoil, a search for balm to bring serenity to the wounded self, "the perturbed spirit," as it were.

The quest for serenity amidst the perturbation of Elsinore is after all a major motif in *Hamlet*. It often surfaces in the midst of the bewildering array of mirror relationships that make up the substance of the text. Harold Jenkins, for example, points out how Laertes actually becomes the "image" of Hamlet (5.2.77) by usurping Hamlet's own role as the wronged son of a wronged father.[25] Hamlet himself thinks he wants to be like Fortinbras, finding "quarrel in a straw" (4.4.55).

Little noticed, however, despite all the commentary on Hamlet's relationship with his father, is that Hamlet can offer no greater gift to his father than serenity of self ("Rest, rest, perturbed spirit" [1.5.182]). The frightful specter of the other world conjured up by the father ("I could a tale unfold whose lightest word / Would harrow up thy soul, freeze thy young blood, / Make thy two eyes . . . start from their spheres, / Thy knotted and combined locks to part" [1.5.15–18]) becomes a blueprint for Hamlet's own torment. He too, like his father, comes to know the serpent's sting of the "adulterate, incestuous beast," the uncle Claudius; the guilt for "foul crimes done in day's of nature" in the deaths of Polonius, Rosencrantz, and Guildenstern; and the terrible uncertainty of finding no peace in the garden even in his "most secure hour." The greatest gift, then, that Hamlet can give to his own father is the identical one he can give to himself—the freedom from perturbation of self.

In multiple ways Duplessis's neo-Stoical treatise on death repeats the same thematic and linguistic patterns found in Hamlet's "To be or not to be" soliloquy, as well as in the duke Vincentio's speech on death in *Measure for Measure*.[26] Indeed, the *Discours*, as translated by the countess of Pembroke, is another of those treatises of consolation that flooded the bookstalls of

Elizabethan England. A good example is Cardan's *Comforte*, which Hardin Craig once took to be "Hamlet's book."[27] At the heart of the credo is theological voluntarism, a willing surrender to the divine will. With Christianized Stoicism comes a sense of serenity, even of liberation, either as consequence or cause of this transcendence of earthly cares. There is also an attitude toward death not as an ending but as a beginning; not the antithesis to but the crowning glory of life; and not the frustration but the consummation of a providential design. Thus Duplessis remarks, "What euill is there in death, that we should so much eschue it? Nay what euill is there not in life?" (sig. A3ʳ);[28] or again, and reminiscent of Hamlet's ruminative voice, "For I pray what can he feare, whose death is his hope? Thinke we to banish him his country? He knows he hath a country other-where, whence wee cannot banish him; and that all these countries are but Innes" (sig. E1ᵛ). With Montaigne, Duplessis shared the motto *Mourir pour vivre, & vivre pour mourir* ("To die to live, and to live to die").

That separation between self-empowerment and institutional disempowerment is finally healed by the end of the play. Sometime after the abortive trip to England and after the symbolic descent into Ophelia's grave, Hamlet locates within himself a power that he no longer can find without. The secular institutions of Elsinore only encourage the cutting of throats in a church. Hamlet paradoxically can carry out his selving in the context of Nature, of mysterious Otherness, an immanent voice that gives him the conviction to find meaning in the smallest act, even in "the fall of a sparrow." In Duplessis's words, the *topos* emerges this way: "God calleth home from his work, one in the morning, an other at noone, and an other at night . . . euery one in his time. Who leaues his worke before God call him, looses it; and who importunes him before the time, looses his reward. We must rest us in his will, who in the middest of our troubles sets us at rest" (sig. E2ᵛ).

Hamlet's new self-empowerment, though powerless in the eyes

of secularized, Renaissance man, is supreme in the eyes of a reformist God. It simultaneously transcends and subverts secular models of behavior to find an inner strength of unparalleled force. Indeed, it plays a variation on the Pauline doctrine of the "Holy Fool," the person wise in the eyes of god who is foolish in the eyes of man (see 1 Cor. 1:18–19). Again, Duplessis puts it this way: "We looke, but through false spectacles: we haue eyes but ouergrowen with pearles: we thinke we see, but it is in a dreame" (sig. D4ʳ). This freshly tapped moral armor, which now makes him conciliatory rather than vengeful toward former enemies, with the apparent exception of Claudius (though no one really knows what might have happened if Claudius had not initiated his counter–revenge plot), allows Hamlet to resolve the ultimate dilemma of whether "to be" or "not to be." In the mind of Duplessis, "to be" and "not to be," in the Aristotelian sense of "being" and "nonbeing," stood for life and death: "It remaineth then that not beeing, not Living . . . were afore Beeing." [29] For Hamlet "to be" was to confront the challenge not only of the world below in Elsinore but also the world above of his father's spirit. As Duplessis said, "Death only can restore us both light and life" (sig. D4⁺). In death, as it were, Hamlet finds that "light" Claudius and Polonius cry out for (3.2.269) but cannot find. Thus, Hamlet by the end of the play is less the avenger of evil than the instrument of god's justice. [30]

That through the playwright's artistic legerdemain Hamlet's regeneration is couched in virtually secular terms is only a greater tribute to Shakespeare's genius for making the parochial universal. Hamlet, who was already the "glass of fashion," had to locate technologies of self in a new "mould of form" (3.1.153), to replace the one that Ophelia had once spoken of so admiringly. A new self had to be refashioned out of the remnants of an older self. Hamlet could not move between the Machiavellian worldliness of Elsinore and the Protestant zeal of Wittenberg without suffering personal trauma and initiating social disaster. His calamitous solution for suturing the raw edges between self and society may seem to the modern mind only a delaying action, or a nonsolution, for a timeless dilemma. Although neither Hamlet nor Shakespeare could foresee twentieth-century tensions between technologies of society and self, they nevertheless managed to prefigure those tensions. *Hamlet* fixes our gaze upon the order of things as past, present, and future converge. And even if we can never pluck out the heart of Hamlet's mystery, the privilege of contemplating Shakespeare's representation of it endures.

Notes

1   *Hamlet* 3.1.153. This and subsequent quotations from Shakespeare are from *The Riverside Shakespeare*, ed. G. Blakemore Evans et al. (Boston: Houghton Mifflin, 1974).

2   See Stephen Greenblatt, *Renaissance Self-fashioning: From More to Shakespeare* (Chicago: University of Chicago Press, 1980). Most of the figures chosen for inspection in Professor Greenblatt's study had a greater need than Hamlet for "self-fashioning." Hence, in this essay I employ "refashioning" as Hamlet's essential methodology. For an earlier study of "self" in the plays of Shakespeare, see also J. Leeds Barroll, *Artificial Persons: The Formation of Character in the Tragedies of Shakespeare* (Columbia: University of South Carolina Press, 1974). Barroll's concept of "transcendental being" is particularly useful in calibrating the differences between modern and late medieval modes of self-evaluation.

3   Two fairly recent references include Nigel Alexander, *Poison, Play, and Duel: A Study in Hamlet* (Lincoln: University of Nebraska Press, 1971), pp. 8–9; and Walter N. King, *Hamlet's Search for Meaning* (Athens: University of Georgia Press, 1982), p. 17. King remarks, in a way that seems to corroborate the general thrust of this chapter, that "Nowhere else [but at Wittenberg] would Hamlet have been so likely to come into mental contact with providential thinking in all its controversiality."

4   As everyone knows, Tudor religious tracts raised calumny and invective to a high art, which is amply illustrated in the Parker Society publications. For a typical exchange, characteristic in tone and substance, see John G. Jewel, *A Defence of the Apologie of the Church of England, conteining an Answer to a Certain Book lately set forth by Mr. Harding . . .*, in *Works of John Jewel*, vol. 3, ed. John Eyre, Parker Society, 25 (Cambridge: Cambridge University Press, 1848). Harding's

Roman Catholic replies to Bishop Jewel's Anglican accusations are equally vituperative.

5   *Power/Knowledge: Selected Interviews and Other Writings, 1972–77*, by Michel Foucault, ed. Colin Gordon (New York: Pantheon Books, 1980), p. 92.

6   See the pseudonomynous *A Defence of Liberty against Tyrants. A Translation of the Vindiciae Contra Tyrannos by Junius Brutus*, introd. Harold Laski (1924; rpt. Gloucester, Mass.: Smith, 1963), often attributed to Duplessis-Mornay, for an example of a Protestant polemic against the tyranny of kings.

7   S. F. Johnson, "The Regeneration of Hamlet," *Shakespeare Quarterly* 3 (1952): 206.

8   Quoted in Robert S. Westman, "The Melanchthon Circle, Rheticus, and the Wittenberg Interpretation of the Copernican Theory," *Isis* 66 (1975): 170. My thanks to Theodore Chiari, UVM 1986, for steering me toward this article and the one on Peucer cited in note 9.

9   For a summary of Peucer's scholarly interests and place in the Philippist movement at Wittenberg, see Robert Kolb, "Caspar Peucer's Library: Portrait of a Wittenberg Professor of the Mid-Sixteenth Century," *Sixteenth-Century Bibliography* 5 (St. Louis: Center for Reformation Research, 1976).

10   Greenblatt, *Renaissance Self-fashioning*, p. 87.

11   See Huck Gutman, "Rousseau's *Confessions:* A Technology of the Self," paper presented to University of Vermont Faculty Foucault Seminar, fall 1982, and included in this volume as chapter 6. Professor Gutman's analysis of Rousseau highlights the relative reticence of pre-Romantic figures in revealing innermost thoughts of self. As Foucault puts it: "one goes about telling, with the greatest precision, whatever is most difficult to tell" (*The History of Sexuality*, vol. 1: *An Introduction*, trans. Robert Hurley [New York: Pantheon Books, 1978]), p. 59.

12   Harold Jenkins, Introduction, *Hamlet*, The Arden Shakespeare (New York: Methuen, 1982), p. 129.

13   See Kenneth S. Rothwell, "*Hamlet*, Duplessis-Mornay, and the 'Irenic' Vision," *Hamlet Studies* 3 (1981): 13–31.

14   See Foucault's exhaustive analysis in "The Theory of the Verb" for an interesting sidelight on Hamlet's use of "to be." *The Order of Things: An Archaeology of the Human Sciences* (New York: Pantheon, 1965), pp. 92–96.

15   King, *Hamlet's Search for Meaning*, p. 14.

16   Marcus Aurelius, *Meditations*, trans. A. S. L. Farquharson (London: Dent, 1961), pp. 9–10.

17   Ibid., p. 65.

18   This dualism in Hamlet's character has not gone unnoticed by other commentators. Sir John Gielgud mentions that "he [Hamlet] . . . is extremely difficult to reconcile with the violent and far more showy passages in the early scenes," in Rosamond Gilder, *John Gielgud's Hamlet: A Record of Performance* (New

York: Oxford University Press, 1973), p. 52; Joan Rees refers to the "new tone in which Hamlet speaks to Laertes" after the graveyard scene, in *Shakespeare and the Story* (London: Athlone, 1978), p. 191; Maurice Charney observes that "before the sea voyage Hamlet was at a standstill; now he moves with new sureness," in "Reading *Hamlet*: Text, Context, and Subtext," in *How to Read Shakespearean Tragedy*, ed. Edward Quinn (New York: Harper and Row, 1978), p. 130; a brilliant analysis of the problem appeared long ago in Johnson, "Regeneration of Hamlet," where Hamlet is seen as being transformed from "the student prince" to "the ordained minister of providence"; and the latest contribution, a weighty attempt to show the logic of Hamlet's transformation within the framework of modern Christian existentialism, is King's *Hamlet's Search for Meaning*.

19   Foucault, *Madness and Civilization: A History of Insanity in the Age of Reason*, trans. Richard Howard (New York: Pantheon, 1965), p. 33.

20   King's *Hamlet's Search for Meaning* is a sustained search for that artistic design.

21   For documentation of these biographical facts, see Rothwell, *"Hamlet, Duplessis-Mornay."* The correspondence of Duplessis-Mornay, for example, testifies to his friendship with the Sidney family, and his wife's memoirs offer insight into the bond between English and French Protestantism in the sixteenth century. See *Mémoires et correspondance Duplessis-Mornay*, ed. A. D. de la Fontenelle de Vaudoré and P. R. Auguis, 11 vols. (Paris: Iez Treutel et Wurtz, 1824). Vol. 1 contains the memoir by Charlotte Arbaleste Mornay, *A Huguenot Family in the 16th Century . . .*, trans. Lucy Crump (London: Routledge, n.d.).

22   I am obliged here to Jeanne Harrie, "Duplessis-Mornay, Foix-Candale, and the Hermetic Religion of the World," *Renaissance Quarterly* 31 (1978): 499–514, for this insight into the "irenic" temper.

23   Rothwell, *"Hamlet, Duplessis-Mornay."*

24   William Stearns Davis, *A History of France from the Earliest Times to the Treaty of Versailles* (Boston: Houghton Mifflin, 1919), p. 120. I am also obliged for an overview of the Reformation to Will Durant, *The Story of Civilization* (New York: Simon and Schuster, 1935), vol. 7.

25   Jenkins, Introduction, p. 144.

26   Katherine Duncan-Jones, "Stoicism in *Measure for Measure*," *Review of English Studies* 28 (1977): 441–46, explores the links between Duplessis's *Discours* and the speeches on death by the duke Vincentio and Claudio (3.1) in an article that appeared after I had begun my own research into the influence of Duplessis.

27   Hardin Craig, "Hamlet's Book," *Huntington Library Bulletin* 6 (1934): 17–37.

28   Quotations from Duplessis's *Discours* are from the 1592 London edition, translated into English by Mary Sidney and printed by William Ponsonby, a "bookbinder" who often served the Sidney family.

29   "Of the Trewnes of Christian Religion," in *The Prose Works of Sir Philip Sidney*, vol. 3, ed. Albert Feuillerat (Cambridge: Cambridge University Press, 1962), p. 206.

30   Robert G. Hunter, *Shakespeare and the Mystery of God's Judgments* (Athens: University of Georgia Press, 1976), p. 125. Professor Hunter spells out the strong Calvinist energies in Hamlet's behavior: " 'Thy will be done.' Amen, *ainsi soit-il*, let be. Nothing is easier to say or harder to mean and Hamlet's ability to mean it is, for me, the final and indeed the only possible proof of what I must clumsily call his 'election.' "

Six ROUSSEAU'S *Confessions:*

A TECHNOLOGY OF THE SELF

HUCK GUTMAN

> For a long time ordinary individuality—the everyday individuality of
> everybody—remained below the threshold of description.
> FOUCAULT, *Discipline and Punish*

> This turning of real lives into writing is no longer a procedure of
> heroization; it functions as a procedure of objectification and subjection . . .
> the appearance of a new modality of power in which each individual
> receives as his status his own individuality and in which he is linked by his
> status to the features, the measurements, the gaps, the "marks" that
> characterize him and make him a case.
> FOUCAULT, *Discipline and Punish*

> It is very unhappy, but too late to be helped, the discovery we have made
> that we exist. That discovery is called the *Fall of Man* . . . . Life will be
> imaged, but it cannot be divided or doubled. Any invasion of its unity
> would be chaos.
> RALPH WALDO EMERSON, "Experience"

Immanuel Kant was a man of extremely regular habits. Each
afternoon he would go for a walk through the streets of
Koenigsberg. His itinerary was so regular and his pace so precise
that the townsfolk would set their watches by his appearance on
their street. Only twice was Kant's routine interrupted. Once was
on that day when he learned of the storming of the Bastille, the
day that ushered in the French Revolution. The other
interruption was for a period of two or three days, during the
period he was reading Rousseau's *Emile*.

Although we know that Kant was of the opinion that Rousseau was the most remarkable mind of his time, we do not know for certain why he interrupted his fixed and determined routines to read *Emile*. However, it is not difficult to understand, for Rousseau seems to have had a profound effect on almost everyone. Great numbers of people, like Kant, saw Rousseau as the harbinger of great possibilities for human growth and freedom. Not everyone, of course, found Rousseau remarkable or liberatory; many reviled him, so many that it is not unfair to say that no name or person was more hated in Europe from his day forth, until the arrival of a very different sort of person, Adolph Hitler, upon the historical scene. But it was no blood lust that Rousseau satisfied, nor did he promise relief for the anxieties of existence through a commitment to an ideal of racial purity. Rousseau's immense appeal—and the equally enormous disapproval he elicited—was directly owing to his sensibility, to the shape of his perceptions.

What Kant, the philosopher who bound truth to the shape of human perception, responded to in Rousseau seems clear. Rousseau reveals and celebrates the atomistic, autonomous self: He is perhaps the first human being to insist upon his own singularity. "My mind," he says, "needs to go forward in its own time, it cannot submit itself to anyone else's."[1] "For I knew that my experience did not apply to others" (67). He shatters the great paradigm of microcosm and macrocosm. If his life's story has relevance to the reader, it is not because we are all reflections of Rousseau but rather because we are all unique, all selves with our individual histories and idiosyncratic perceptions. Indeed, Rousseau understands his significance is rooted not in his similarity to others but in his "exaggerated sensibility" (235).

Kant must also have responded to a genuinely new conception of the self which shapes Rousseau's presentation of his life, a conception which sees the emotive life as the basis for individuality. "I felt before I thought" (19), Rousseau claims early in his autobiography, emphasizing in one short phrase both the primacy of feeling that was to mark his unique sensibility and the prescient recognition that it is in time, through temporal succession, that the self comes to be what it is.[2] In a famous passage explaining the onset of the physical disabilities that were to plague him for the latter half of his life, Rousseau speaks of a life governed by his emotions:

> The sword wears out its sheath, as it is sometimes said. That is my story. My passions have made me live, and my passions have killed me. What passions, it may be asked. Trifles, the most childish things in the world. Yet they affected me as much as if the possession of Helen, or the throne of the Universe, had been at stake. [199]

Although this valorization of feeling has roots in the Reformation, with its emphasis on the individual as the ultimate hermeneutic authority, it is with Rousseau that a genuinely modern temper, which we call romanticism, first comes clearly into view. Rousseau was the first Romantic.

There is a clear correspondence between the two aspects of Rousseau's sensibility—the emergence of an individuality, a clearly defined *self*, above the threshold of visibility, and the valorization of the emotive life—for the two exist in a reciprocally defining relation. When Rousseau meditates upon the activity he is engaged in, that of writing his life's history, he says:

> I have only one faithful guide on which I can count; the succession of feelings which marked the development of my being, and thereby recall the events that have acted upon it as cause or effect. I easily forget my misfortunes [this is in fact not the case, despite his claim] but I cannot forget my faults, and still less my genuine feelings. The memory of them is too dear ever to be effaced from my heart. I may omit or transpose

facts, or make mistakes in dates; but I cannot go wrong about what I have felt, or about what my feelings have led me to do; and these are the chief subjects of my story. The true object of my confessions is to reveal my inner thoughts exactly in all the situations of my life. It is the history of my soul that I have promised to recount, and to write it faithfully I have need of no other memories; it is enough if I enter again into my inner self, as I have done till now. [262]

What Rousseau "confesses" is that he is who he is—an individuated self whom he calls "Jean-Jacques"—because he has had a succession of emotions prior to, interwoven with, and resultant from his interactions with the world. And, as we shall see, it is not accidental that the emergence of this feeling and individuated self is connected to, and dependent on, the activity of writing.

In order to understand what Rousseau was doing, and also what he was *not* doing, in his *Confessions*, we must look back to Augustine, bishop of Hippo. In 397, Saint Augustine wrote his *Confessions*, a work that in retrospect we might call a spiritual autobiography. Augustine lays before his readers the chronicle of his spiritual waywardness and his eventual turn toward the church and the service of God. But calling this project a spiritual autobiography is misleading in two respects. First, Augustine is not primarily concerned with *his* spirit, and second, although he recounts the episodes of his life that are important to his purpose, his purpose itself is not to tell the story of his life. What Augustine does is use his own experience as an *exemplum* of the glory of God and the workings of His spirit. Augustine, it is true, recounts his specific experience of stealing pears from a tree and his own strong attraction toward carnal knowledge of women, but he relates these episodes in order to show how even the least worthy of human beings can still discover the grace of God, whose mercy and forgiveness is available even to such a debased creature as the libertine Augustine once was. Any modern reader of Augustine's *Confessions* is struck by how little Augustine, and how much revelation of God's work, it contains. Although the *Confessions* is an enormously important work in that history of the gradual emergence of a visible self, its importance arises from the inclusion of individual experiences and personal shame as an exemplum of God's ability to rescue sinners from their life of sin. That Augustine committed his life and actions and his feelings to writing, so that they might be observed by his readers (and himself), was of signal importance to the Western tradition; on the other hand, nowhere in his *Confessions* does one find Augustine celebrating either himself or his own autonomy. The revelation of self, as it is hesitatingly presented in Augustine, is solely a vehicle to a higher end, which is the glorification of God's beneficence and mercy.

How different are Rousseau's *Confessions*! The purpose here is secular, not religious: It is not to glorify God and urge devotion to Him as the proper course for human beings. Rather, Rousseau's purpose is twofold: to unburden himself of his shame, to reveal himself in his weakness ("One goes about telling, with the greatest precision, whatever is most difficult to tell," as Foucault puts it),[3] and to create a "self" which can serve to define himself, to himself and to others, in the face of a hostile social order. This defined self is what Michel Foucault has so thoroughly and eloquently shown to be a historically produced phenomenon in *Discipline and Punish* and *The History of Sexuality*, the "immense labor . . . to produce . . . men's subjection: their constitution as subjects in both senses of the word."[4] Let me here state explicitly the central theme of my argument: If there has indeed been an immense labor to turn man into a subject (an individuated self and a defined personage in the social order) in order to subject him more completely and inescapably to the traversals and furrowings of power—and I think Foucault has conclusively shown that this is indeed the case—then Rousseau's psyche and in particular his *Confessions* have provided an indispensable *techne* for the elaboration of this labor.

Here is Foucault on the modern confession, and on the revolution in its use ushered in by Rousseau in this regard:

> Western man has become a confessing animal. Whence a metamorphosis in literature: we have passed from a pleasure to be recounted and heard, centering on the heroic or marvelous narration of "trials" of bravery or sainthood, to a literature ordered according to the infinite task of extracting from the depths of oneself, in between the words, a truth which the very form of the confession holds out like a shimmering mirage. . . . The confession is a ritual of discourse in which the speaking subject is also the subject of the statement.[5]

For Augustine, the self as exemplum is ancillary to the discourse. For Rousseau, the self is the subject of the discourse. His aim is not to glorify God but to provide the truth about himself by revealing himself *in all his completeness* to the gaze of the reader. "I never promised to present the public with a great personage. I promised to depict myself as I am. . . . I should like in some way to make my soul transparent to the reader's eye. . . . so that he may judge for himself of the principle which has produced them [the various dimensions of his soul]" (169).

Rousseau opens his *Confessions* by addressing his potential readers:

> I have resolved on an enterprise which has no precedent, and which, once complete, will have no imitator. My purpose is to display to my kind a portrait in every way true to nature, and the man I shall portray will be myself.
>
> Simply myself. I know my own heart and understand my fellow man. . . .

So let the numberless legion of my fellow men gather round
me, and hear my confessions. [17]

His method will be openness, what he calls "frank treatment: I
decided to make it a work unique and unparalleled in its
truthfulness, so that for once at least the world might behold a
man as he was within" (478). The lever that propels him into this
activity of committing his life to words, and his words to writing
so that they may be subjected to the gaze of his public, has, as it
were, a dual fulcrum. First, there is Rousseau's remorse (and here
we might note a parallel to Augustine). In referring to the lie he
told about a ribbon he stole, a lie that destroyed the integrity of
an innocent fellow servant, Rousseau observes that "I took away
with me lasting memories of a crime and the unbearable weight of
a remorse" (86). Confession relieves this weight. "The desire to
some extent to rid myself of it has greatly contributed to my
resolution of writing these *Confessions*" (88). And the process of
writing, of exposing oneself,[6] is not only a relief but a pleasure.
"Such were the errors and faults of my youth," he writes. "I have
told the story of them with a fidelity that brings pleasure to my
heart." Motivated by guilt and shame and remorse, having
discovered a secular form of the religious practice of confession
that brought alleviation from such self-mortifying emotions, it is
no wonder that Rousseau acknowledged that "a continuous need
to pour myself out brings my heart at every moment to my lips
[to] . . . confess unreservedly" (152).

The other fulcrum of Rousseau's need to confess becomes
increasingly apparent in the later, darker books of the *Confessions*.
Betrayed by his friends, reviled by what seemed an entire
continent, Rousseau confesses in order to justify his existence. He
would constitute a self, in writing, as he feels his self to be. And
he will hold this self up as an alternative before the gaze of a
public that has only been able to see a Rousseau who is asocial,
self-serving, immoral, and dangerous.

In order to defend himself against the grand conspiracy that tries to demean him everywhere, Rousseau must create himself as a character with a history. He must exhibit everything, expose himself completely before the public gaze. He must reveal every aspect and activity of his life, even the

> petty details . . . since I have undertaken to *reveal myself absolutely* to the public, nothing about me must remain hidden or obscure. *I must remain incessantly beneath his gaze*, so that he may follow me in all the extravagances of my heart and into every least corner of my life. Indeed, he must *never lose sight of me for a single instant*, for if he finds the smallest gap in my story, the smallest hiatus, he may wonder what I was doing at that moment and *accuse me* of refusing to tell the whole truth. I am laying myself sufficiently open. [65; emphases mine]

So we see that Rousseau's confession develops as a response to social accusation, that it consists in total exposure, and that its revelations are to be subjected to an external (and judging) gaze. This process of self-exposure rules the shape and structure of the *Confessions*. Time and again Rousseau refers to this triumvirate of compunction, external gaze, and the need for complete disclosure:

> A change in my relations with Mamma, of which I must speak, since, after all, I must tell everything. [184]

> [There is] my indispensable duty to fulfill it in its entirety. . . . If I am to be known I must be known in all situations, both good and bad. [373]

> [In] my memoir . . . will be found . . . the heart of Jean-Jacques, which my contemporaries have been so unwilling to recognize. [585]

This major shift in consciousness has taken place in the many centuries that separate Rousseau from Augustine. It is a shift that

Professor Foucault has addressed in his contribution to this volume.

Nowhere is the new consciousness that has emerged more apparent than in the sense of division that structures Rousseau's world. If we are to understand his sensibility, his celebration of the self and of feelings, it is toward an examination of these divisions that we must turn.

In order for a man or woman to be constituted as a subject, he or she must first be divided from the totality of the world, or the totality of the social body. For a "me" to emerge, a distinction must be made between the "me" and the "not-me." The boundaries of the self are those lines that divide the self from all that which is not the self, which is beyond the self. The first, and essential, move in the constitution of the self is division.[7]

And it is division, above all, that we discover in Rousseau. Division is the primary move in the countless analyses he provides as the explanation of the course of his existence. Rousseau divides, and then sees opposition between, head and heart; reason and emotion; nature and society; self and society; country and city; and self and nature.

It is this act of dividing that creates the two elements of his sensibility as he presents it. Rousseau's time had already divided the head from the rest of the body: It was, after all, the Age of Reason. What Rousseau did, following the cult of sentimentality that was his precursor, was rebel against the overvaluation of reason by asserting the claims of the emotions.[8]

This dividing strategy is the base of Rousseau's strength. In dividing himself from the world, he creates a self, he constitutes himself as a subject of knowledge and examination. He will explore, in the *Confessions*, the particular experiences he has had and, out of those experiences, he will trace the development and boundaries of his own, particular, consciousness. The modern secular confessional, as invented by Rousseau, involves not merely the recital of sins but the enumeration of each and every experience that has made one what and who one is.

In the process of examining the division of the self and the world, Rousseau creates the Romantic paradigm: the recounting of the history of the self so that the self can concurrently create itself in writing and affirm that self it has created. "I am made unlike anyone I have ever met; I will even venture to say that I am like no one in the whole world" (17).

So substantial is the self he has created that he can treat that self as some sort of external object to be examined, as a thing with existence apart from his consciousness. I refer here to Rousseau's strange work, *Rousseau Juge de Jean-Jacques*,[9] a dialogue—Foucault calls it "anti-Confessions"—in which a nameless Frenchman, a representative of the public gaze, subjects Jean-Jacques to an inquisition. Rousseau's "self" has become an object; it has become the subject of this investigation (inquisition). There is a clear relation in this colloquy between two forms of being a subject (a subject to be discussed, a subject in the political sense of being in an inferior relation to power) and a third form, in which the self recognizes it has its own subjectivity.

Nowhere is the self Rousseau has created by the dividing strategy, a self disparate from the world of nature and society, more in evidence than in the paranoid stance that marks his later works. The grand conspiracy that emerges as his constant theme in the second half of the *Confessions*, in the *Dialogues*, and in the *Reveries*, is the structural result of that move Rousseau made in dividing himself out from the rest of the world.[10] Having separated self from other, it is no surprise that Rousseau discovers that the other is alien and, ultimately, inhospitable.

In order to understand that inhospitality more closely we might profitably examine Rousseau's reaction to the appearance of a rival at the ménage of Mme. de Warens. Mme. de Warens—"Mamma," as Rousseau called her— provided Rousseau with the home for which he longed. Protectress, support, and ultimately sexual partner, Mamma was Rousseau's bulwark against the world. When the remarkable domestic triangle of Mme. de Warens, her older lover Claude Anet, and Rousseau, that symbolic family of which he says, possibly accurately, "between the three of us was established a bond perhaps unique on this earth" (194), was disrupted by the death of Anet and the temporary departure of Rousseau, the space occupied by the two men—and that of Rousseau in particular—was filled by a stranger, Vintzenreid. Rousseau's place, both in Mamma's affections and in her bed, was taken by this young rival. Returning to Les Charmettes and confronting the new domestic order, Rousseau describes his predicament: "Insensibly I found myself isolated and alone in that same house of which I had formerly been the centre, and in which I now led, so to speak, a double life" (252).

If we read these words as extending beyond the confines of his particular situation in the household of Mamma, we stand before another major constituent of Rousseau's sensibility. "I found myself isolated and alone." Having divided the "me" from the "not-me," the "me" discovers itself apart, separated, isolated, alone. The world of totality, which was sundered in order to form a new whole, an individuated self, is no longer a totality. As we read this passage symbolically, we see the comforting centrality of the constituted self giving way to isolation and loneliness. Although the first reward of constituting oneself as a subject is a feeling of centrality and well-being, an inevitable consequence of that constitution, which depends upon division, is isolation. All selves lead double lives as object as well as subject (to be a subject is to be able to see oneself as an object); to know the fullness of the self is to encounter the seeming poverty of the world from which that self has been sundered, and out of whose plenitude the self has been filled. It is not surprising that Rousseau finds his internal division "has throughout my life set me in conflict with myself" (23).

Divided by the individuating process from the social world, Rousseau recognizes that an "exaggerated sensibility" contributes powerfully to his growing paranoia. "I was in the most unbearable position for a man whose imagination is easily set working" (458). Such paranoia is but an extension of that primary move that divides self from the world and places the self above that from which it has been separated. Rousseau's imagination—that central agent of the Romantic sensibility—is here acknowledged as a force in the emergence and expansion of his paranoid sense of a grand conspiracy that is marshaled against him.

But the role of the imagination, the power of the individual mind to create and re-create the world, is not limited to the expanding vision of an alien, dangerous, and ultimately persecutory world. The role of imagination in Rousseau's sensibility is dialectical: While it expands the inhospitable, it creates for itself at the same time a bulwark against this inhospitality. The imagination, which exaggerates the isolation and estrangement of the solitary consciousness that has separated itself off from the world, also domesticates a new (imaginary) world, so that the unhappy consciousness can regain, through the workings of the imaginative power of re-creation, what it has lost, so that it can once again be at home in the world.

Early in the *Confessions* Rousseau recounts his experience as an apprentice. Denied both autonomy and a sense that the small world he inhabits is his home, he feels deprived; and deprivation leads to the attempt to find satisfaction in what might be called "devious" ways. "Because I was deprived of everything," Rousseau informs the reader, "so it was that I learnt to covet in silence, to conceal, to dissimulate, to lie, and finally to steal" (40). This structure—deprivation succeeded by the attempt to regain that of which he is deprived—underlies later, more profound developments in Rousseau's stance toward the world.

Rousseau turns to the workings of his imagination because the imagination can supply the lack he feels. Shortly after the passage about stealing cited above, Rousseau observes his youthful self "tenderly nursing my illusions . . . since I saw nothing around me

I valued as much" (49). He speaks as well of his absorption in books, and this leads him to make this revealing statement: "The fictions I succeeded in building up *made me forget my real condition*, which so dissatisfied me" (48; emphasis mine). Rousseau is explicit later in the first part of the *Confessions*:

> It is a very strange thing that my imagination never works more delightfully than when my situation is the reverse of delightful, and that, on the other hand, it is never less cheerful than when all is cheerful around me. It cannot beautify; it must create. . . . as I have said a hundred times, if every I were confined in the Bastille, there I would draw the picture of liberty. [166]

Nowhere is the relation between deprivation and the imagination clearer than in Rousseau's description of the creation of *La Nouvelle Héloïse*:

> The impossibility of attaining the real persons precipitated me into the land of chimeras; and seeing nothing that existed worthy of my exalted feelings, I fostered them in an ideal world which my creative imagination soon peopled with beings after my own heart. . . . altogether ignoring the human race, I created for myself societies of perfect creatures. [398]

So strong is his imagination, so powerful are the figures that it creates, that Rousseau ends up transforming the actual personages he encounters into the fleshly counterparts of the "chimeras" he has been creating. Rousseau wrote *La Nouvelle Héloïse* because he had never felt a full and satisfying love (he claims) in his life, and because he had never met a woman fine enough to elicit such a love from him. It should be no surprise, considering his penchant for the imagination—he says he was unimpressed on first entering Paris "for it is impossible for me, and difficult for Nature herself, to surpass the riches of my imagination" (155)—that, after having created the "chimera" of Julie, that imagination would re-create the "real world" so that he could encounter her in his daily, bodily life. His imagination transforms, and re-creates, reality (Rousseau refers here to the grand passion of his life, his love for Mme. d'Houdetot):

> She came; I saw her; I was intoxicated with love that lacked an object. My intoxication enchanted my eyes, my object became identified with her, I saw Julie in Mme. d'Houdetot and soon I saw only Mme. d'Houdetot. [410]

So deficient reality is transformed into the imaginary, and the imaginary is superimposed upon the real in such fashion that the imaginary transforms, takes over, becomes, the real.

This double displacement, of the real into the imaginary and the imaginary into the real, raises difficult questions, which the reader of the *Confessions* must address. If the imaginary first displaces and then replaces the real, to what extent can the reader trust what Rousseau has to say about himself throughout his autobiography?[11] Given Rousseau's continual flight from deprivation and reality into the imaginary, is it not possible that the *Confessions* itself is a fiction created to remedy this deprivation, to hold the pressures of the actual at bay? And, further, is it not possible that "Jean-Jacques Rousseau" is a character, his self a "chimera," his subjectivity a construct?

Rousseau helps the reader to answer such questions in the affirmative by time and again referring to the fictive quality of his narrative. On the very first page of the *Confessions*, four sentences after saying "My purpose is to display to my kind a portrait in every way true to nature, and the man I shall portray is myself," Rousseau indicates that this is indeed a *portrait*, an imaginative construct: "I may have taken for fact what was no more than probability, but I have never put down as true what I knew to be false" (17). In other words, the self he puts before us may very well be made up! Although we can say that the self that has emerged above the threshold of visibility in Rousseau chooses to celebrate its own power to create and re-create the world, we can say with equal justice that the sensibility that seeks a recourse to the world in which it discovers itself chooses to invent a self as a refuge from, and bulwark against, that world. Encountering the complexities of social existence, the real fact of human oppression, the limits of human possibility, Rousseau in some sense "creates" himself as Jean-Jacques, as a subject who can discover in his subjectivity an escape from, and an alternative to, these conditions.

Let us shift the object of Rousseau's description of his encounter with Mme. d'Houdetot from that erstwhile lady to Rousseau himself. If we make the appropriate substitutions, that passage then reads, "Jean-Jacques came; I saw myself; I was intoxicated with need that lacked an object. My intoxication enchanted my eyes, my object became identified with myself, I saw Rousseau in Jean-Jacques and soon I saw only Jean-Jacques." It is indeed possible that the celebration of the self in the *Confessions* is a narrative similar in structure to the creation of Julie, and its effect on Rousseau's actual daily existence is similar to the superimposition of Julie on Mme. d'Houdetot. It is indeed possible that, having divided the world into self and not-self, the embrace and celebration of self is yet another instance of Rousseau's flight from reality into the imaginary. The self, then, is fetishized, the object of desire which is wished into being.

Yet it is one of the very great ironies of Rousseau's autobiographical, confessional *oeuvre* that its central strategy, the dividing off of self from not-self and the consequent exploration and celebration of that self, is eventually negated. The individuated self of Rousseau finally proves ineffective, the deprivation it entails finally overcomes the compensatory satisfactions it produces, and Rousseau ends up annihilating—or desiring to annihilate—the very boundaries of the self that his confessional works seek to impose.

I refer here to the remarkable passage in Rousseau's last work,

The Reveries of a Solitary Walker,[12] where in the "Fifth Walk" Rousseau abandons the active self, erases the boundaries between self and not-self, and surrenders to a totality that would seem to replicate that unity which preceded the division of experience into self and not-self. In this walk, Rousseau meditates on his short stay on Saint Peter's Island in the Lake of Bienne in Switzerland.

Readers of the *Confessions* are prepared for this astonishing meditation, for Rousseau, in stating that "True happiness is indescribable; it can only be felt, and the stronger the feeling the less it can be described, because it is not the result of a collection of facts but a permanent state" (224), had indicated that experience somehow transcends categories and divisions. Indeed, that passage denies the stated method of his autobiographical form—the attempt to recount every detail of his life—in suggesting that existence is more than the sum of the statements one can make about it. Later, the "permanent state" is equated with the asocial and undirected activity of the young and the aged in a passage that attempts to describe his feeling of happiness on Saint Peter's Island:

> The idleness I love is not that of an indolent fellow who stands with folded arms in perfect inactivity, and thinks as little as he acts. It is the idleness of a child who is incessantly on the move without ever doing anything, and at the same time it is the idleness of a rambling old man whose mind wanders while his arms are still. . . . I love . . . to fritter away the whole day inconsequentially and incoherently, and to follow nothing but the whim of the moment. [591–92]

Ten years after he wrote this in the *Confessions* he returned to the same subject—his happiness on Saint Peter's Island—in the "Fifth Walk" of the *Reveries*:

> When evening approached, I would come down from the heights of the island and gladly go sit in some hidden nook

along the beach at the edge of the lake. There, the noise of the waves and the tossing of the water, captivating my senses and chasing all other disturbance from my soul, plunged it into a delightful reverie in which night would often surprise me without my having noticed it. The ebb and flow of this water and its noise, continual but magnified at intervals, striking my ears and eyes without respite, took the place of the internal movements which reverie extinguished within me and was enough to make me feel my existence with pleasure and without taking the trouble to think. From time to time some weak and short reflection about the instability of things in this world arose, an image brought on by the surface of the water. But soon these weak impressions were erased by the uniformity of the continual movement which lulled me and which, without any active assistance from my soul, held me so fast that, called by the hour and agreed-upon signal, I could not tear myself away without effort. . . .

What do we enjoy in such a situation? Nothing external to ourselves, nothing if not ourselves and our own existence. As long as this state lasts, we are sufficient unto ourselves, like God. The sentiment of existence, stripped of any other emotion, is in itself a precious sentiment of contentment and peace which alone would suffice to make this existence dear and sweet to anyone able to spurn all the sensual and earthly impressions which incessantly come to distract us from it and to trouble its sweetness here-below. But most men, agitated by continual passions, are little acquainted with this state and, having tasted it only imperfectly for a few moments, preserve only an obscure and confused idea of it which does not let them feel its charm.[13]

What we see in these passages is a stunning convergence. By abandoning himself *entirely* to his reverie, to the imaginary, the imagining *self* is annihilated, and the self and nature, me and not-me, are merged into an undifferentiated and undivided unity.

Freud, who called this state, referring to its ubiquitous
appearance as a variety of religious experience, the "oceanic
feeling," a phrase one imagines Rousseau would have found
felicitious, sees in this "oceanic feeling" the requited desire of the
ego for a loss of itself, for its undifferentiated merge into the
cosmos. [14]

Thus, Rousseau in the *Confessions* intuits, and in the *Reveries*
discovers, that the created self, the division of self from the
world, is a strategic move finally incapable of engendering human
happiness. The profound irony is this: The great architect of the
modern self ends up discovering that the building he has
constructed is, when it comes right down to it, uninhabitable.
The imaginary, into which the self has retreated as its protection
from the world, ends up by discarding the self and merging, in
unmediated fashion, into the totality of things.

Yet, despite Rousseau's ultimate dissatisfaction with the self he
had done so much to create and differentiate, the reader of the
Confessions understands that its immense significance, its aura of
newness, has to do with its documentation of the emergence of
that subject which was theretofore largely hidden: "For a long
time ordinary individuality—the everyday individuality of
everybody—remained below the threshold of description." [15]
What Rousseau does is take an essential step toward lowering this
threshold: He describes himself, his individuality. He invents (or,
in some senses, he elaborates and extends) several vital techniques
in the constitution of the self as a subject. We have seen these
techniques and the role they play in the *Confessions*:

1. The emergence of the unique, individuated self as a subject of
   observation and description
2. The division of human experience into self and other, me and
   not-me, individual and society
3. The emergence of the self as object of the gaze of the other,
   the public: what Foucault might call the self under examination
4. The development of the (secular) confessional mode of consti-

tuting the self by writing it, with its Rousseauian stress on
completeness, on the inclusion of every detail

5. The dissatisfaction with these four techniques and their results,
    which leads to the valorization of the imaginary—only to cul-
    minate in the final annihilation, by the imaginary, of the self,
    division, the gaze, and writing

The importance of these first four techniques (we shall return to
the fifth presently) cannot be overestimated. Rousseau helps to
invent—and to justify and to circulate—those techniques which
constitute the modern subject. The emergent self becomes the
locus on which, through which, in which, the technology of
power that Professor Foucault has traced will elaborate and invent
itself.[16] If we apply his three modes of constituting the subject
both as object of power and as the self-recognized subject of
power,[17] we see all three at work in the *Confessions*. Rousseau
constitutes the self as subject by objectivizing the speaking subject
in language, by presenting him to the gaze of the knowledgeable
reader. He objectivizes the subject by means of division. And he
refines a technique (the written confession) by means of which the
self comes to recognize itself as subject, and object.

Rousseau develops a technology of the self which, although not
as yet observedly traversed by power, was shortly to become a
prime agent in the modern elaboration of power. Rousseau brings
the self above the threshold of visibility, and he provides several
means by which this self can be made subject.

But if Rousseau is an unwitting agent in the elaboration of the
technology of power, it must also be remembered that he is,
ironically, also a prime agent in the emergence of a new and
powerful opposition to regnant power. Just as the creation and
celebration of his own self contained the imperative that led to
that self's annihilation, so the creation of a public self subject to
the microphysics of power gave rise to a counterforce that would
oppose all regnant power. In the *Confessions* we encounter
everywhere the sense of deprivation which, I have argued, is

generated by that very division that constitutes the self. Because
the self comes into being simultaneously with the perception of
lack and loss, that emergence is everywhere linked to conditions
the self must refuse to accept.

Yet, as Rousseau's constitution of the self has had historical
ramifications, as the forms and techniques of knowledge that he
developed have been traversed by power, so also his deprivation
and refusal to be deprived have had political and historical effects.
The very self that has been created by division, by the abundance
of detail amassed about its activities, by its subjection to the
public gaze and the public judgment, this constituted self
generates not only its subjection but also an opposition to such
subjection, a movement toward liberation.

The spirit of Rousseau is, after all, the spirit of the French
Revolution. It was Rousseau who said, "I had seen that
everything is rooted in politics" (377). It was Rousseau who
would claim of the knowledge/power relation, "I could see only
foolishness and error in the doctrines of our sages, nothing but
oppression and misery in our social order" (387). And, finally, it
was the very self that Rousseau helped to create that became the
basis for the revolutionary desire to transform society so that it
would be conducive to the liberty and equality of all men and
women, each of whom possessed their own individuality.

Thus, the emergence of the modern self, the self as subject, figures
prominently in the subjection of humankind, and figures prominently in
the genesis of those modern struggles that seek, in the face of that
subjection, to reclaim their humanity for men and women.

Notes

1   *The Confessions of Jean-Jacques Rousseau* was completed in 1765 and first
published in 1781. The English translation is by J. M. Cohen (Harmondsworth:
Penguin Books, 1953), p. 118. Subsequent quotations from this edition will be
cited parenthetically in the text.

2   See Michel Foucault, *The Order of Things: An Archaeology of the Human*

Sciences (New York: Pantheon Books, 1970), where the constitutive principle of the episteme of the nineteenth and early twentieth centuries is shown to be temporality and causation. Rousseau's stress on his own development is thus a key element in the transition from an Enlightenment episteme based on mathesis, or spatial placement, to the barely emergent episteme of the later period.

3   Michel Foucault, *The History of Sexuality*, vol. 1: *An Introduction*, trans. Robert Hurley (New York: Pantheon, 1978), p. 59.

4   Ibid., p. 60.

5   Ibid., pp. 59, 61.

6   One notes in this regard that Rousseau's early sexuality manifested itself in the desire to expose himself to public view. One can only surmise about the possible relations between Rousseau's purported early sexual practice and his later embrace of confessional self-exposure.

7   See J. H. van den Berg, *Divided Existence and Complex Society* (Pittsburgh: Duquesne University Press, 1974). Van den Berg develops his analysis in the context of scientific procedures that originated in the eighteenth century, procedures he sees as ultimately constitutive of a new sense of self. See also his *Changing Nature of Man: Introduction to a Historical Psychology*, trans. H. F. Croes (New York: Norton, 1961). Van den Berg, although he utilizes a phenomenological method different from Foucault's somewhat structural approach, is engaged in a project with many similarities to Foucault's work on the technologies of the self.

8   It is important to note that Rousseau was himself an Enlightenment figure. Despite the stress on his emotive life in the *Confessions*, he still highly values the clarity of thought so prized in the Age of Reason: "Feelings come quicker than lightning and fill my soul, but they bring me no illumination [as thought and reason do]; they burn and dazzle me. I feel everything and see nothing" (113).

9   *Rousseau Juge de Jean-Jacques* (Paris: Colin, 1962). The introduction to this modern edition of the *Dialogues*, as the work is also known, is by Michel Foucault. In it Foucault emphasizes both Rousseau's creation of the Romantic self ("a pattern that is unified and at the same time unique") and the subsequent dissolution of that self ("the dissociated subject, superimposed on himself, a lacuna whom one can only call present by a sort of addition never achieved: as if he appears at a distant vanishing point which only a certain convergence allows the reader to ascertain"), pp. xv–xvi; translation mine.

10   These late works are often described, appropriately, as paranoid. Paranoia, the delusion of self-reference, is but an exaggeration of the self as arbiter of order, value, and meaning. That concept of self has its roots in the Reformation's stress on the individual's unmediated relation to God and reaches an apotheosis in the Romantic era, when the self replaced divinity as the arbiter of order, value, and

meaning. Paranoia would seem to be a historically defined disorder, for it is dependent upon the development of the sense of self that came into being with Rousseau and the Romantics. The paranoid stance derives not from some erroneous sense of self but from an *exaggerated* notion of the importance of the Romantic self.

11   Rousseau has anticipated these questions. It is, after all, he who speaks of the "labour" required by writing the self: "Some of my paragraphs I have shaped and reshaped mentally for five or six nights before they were fit to be put down on paper" (114). It is he who warns us that "Being forced to speak in spite of myself, I am also obliged to conceal myself, to be cunning, to try to deceive" (263).

12   Rousseau, *Les Rêveries du promeneur solitaire* (1776–78; pub. posthumously 1782), trans. Charles E. Butterworth (New York: Harper, 1982).

13   Ibid., 67–69.

14   Freud, *Civilization and Its Discontents* (1930), in *The Standard Edition*, vol. 21 (London: Hogarth, 1961).

15   Foucault, *Discipline and Punish*, trans. Alan Sheridan (New York: Pantheon, 1977), p. 191.

16   The traversing of the individual by power has been the subject of much of Foucault's later work. *Discipline and Punish* investigates the ways in which individuals have been subjected by the gaze of the other. *The History of Sexuality* examines the place of confession in making man and woman into subjects. Michel Foucault, *Power and Knowledge: Selected Interviews and Other Writings, 1972–1977*, ed. Colin Gordon (New York: Pantheon, 1980), pursues the notion that "the history which bears and determines us has the form of a war rather than that of a language: relations of power, not relations of meaning."

17   In a lecture at a conference on "Knowledge, Power, History: Interdisciplinary Approaches to the Works of Michel Foucault" (University of Southern California, October 31, 1981), Foucault stated that his aim "is to create a history of the different modes by which the human being has been made a subject." This historical process, he explained, takes three forms: the objectivizing of the speaking subject by the sciences of language, work, and life; the objectivizing of the subject by the dividing practices; and the self-objectification whose workings become visible when one examines the historical struggles "against a technique, a form of power, which applies to everyday life, attaches him [the individual subject] to his identity, attaches a load of truth to him which he and others must recognize," which in short makes him both a subject to power and an object to himself. Portions of the lecture have been reprinted as part of an essay, "The Subject and Power," *Critical Inquiry* 8 (1982): 777–97.

Seven FOUCAULT, FREUD, AND THE

TECHNOLOGIES OF THE SELF

PATRICK H. HUTTON

Michel Foucault's intellectual odyssey is not unlike the history of the topics he has studied. Both take unexpected turns. Foucault has ranged from historical investigations of insane asylums to prisons, to sexual issues, to techniques of self-care. Yet a continuous path runs through this historical journey that concerns the making of the human mind, a subject that invites discussion of Foucault's relationship to Sigmund Freud. Foucault never discussed the significance of Freud's work in any depth. His remarks consist of scattered and usually oblique references.[1] Yet Foucault's work is heavy with Freud's unstated presence. His authorship, considered in its ensemble, might be interpreted as an apostrophe to Freud, for their methods of approaching the mind are diametrically opposed. Whereas Freud provides a method for investigating the internal workings of the psyche, Foucault seeks to show how the method itself is an ancient technique of self-fashioning that has over the centuries shaped the mind externally. Our conception of the psyche, Foucault contends, has been sculpted by the techniques that we have devised to probe its secrets, to oblige it to give up hidden knowledge that will reveal to us the truth about who we are. Psychoanalysis is from a historical perspective a late addition to that enterprise, born of a long but erratic lineage of techniques for the care of the self.

In the exception he takes to this, the dominant interpretation about mind in Western culture in the twentieth century, Foucault aligns himself with a growing number of historians who are approaching historical psychology from nonpsychoanalytic perspectives. His historical studies have many affinities with those of the new historians of collective mentalities, who deal with the problem of the psyche in terms of its definition by the social and cultural forces with which it is intermeshed. Such historians study the way in which the material environment, social customs, and linguistic usage create a collective psychological milieu in which the individual mind is immersed. The organization of the psyche, they contend, is integrally related to the organization of this network of cultural conventions. If the making of culture is a creative process, it is also a prescriptive one in that the vocabularies we employ and the institutions through which we act provide patterns that set boundaries and give direction to future creative effort. Cultural development, therefore, implies cultural constraint, and the repression with which Freud's psychoanalytic theory seeks to deal is itself born of the rigorous social demands and highly nuanced psychological controls imposed in the complex early-twentieth-century civilization in which he devised his theory.[2]

Freud's work, in contrast, has customarily been interpreted in light of the problems of late-nineteenth-century medicine or, more remotely, the insights of early-nineteenth-century Romantic philosophy.[3] Freud wished to bring the mysteries of the human soul, previously the preserve of poets and theologians, into the realm of scientific understanding. The theory of psychoanalysis that he devised to accomplish that task is based on a model of a tripartite psyche in which the self (ego) wrestles with the conflicts between the drives of unconscious impulses (id) for free expression and the demands of conscience (superego) for their renunciation. The ego's capacity to maintain its identity depends on its ability to sort out these conflicting claims and to make decisions about which to heed and which to deny. The repression of the instinctual desires pressed upon the ego by the id has its social virtues in that the energy of impulses denied may be sublimated into creative and socially useful endeavor. But such conflicts can also promote irresolution and the breakdown of the ego's capacity to assert its authority. The remedy for Freud is to search out the hidden sources of the conflict and so to discover the conditions under which the ego can recover its power.[4]

Such a project is effectively a search for a lost self, which Freud believed was formed yet largely forgotten as a consequence of the psyche's encounter with early life experience. One's sense of identity is forged out of the behavioral patterns established through the psyche's reckoning with particular experiences, especially those of childhood. The way in which the psyche has dealt with experiences in the past sets the course for its dealings with experience in the present. The earlier the reckoning, the more profound its influence. One's sense of self is thus shaped by powerful precedents out of the past.[5] The problem is that the psyche's capacity to resolve the conflict between the countervailing demands of the id for instinctual gratification and of the superego for their denial can never be perfectly reconciled. Confronted with such choices, human beings cannot expect to attain enduring happiness. They can at best mitigate unhappiness, for human nature contains flaws that cannot be eliminated.[6] The painful choices and unresolved conflicts with which all of us are confronted, therefore, are often repressed in the unconscious mind. Forgotten by the ego, they remain hidden yet active problems that trouble the unconscious mind. Not only is the psyche in the present bound to the unresolved issues of its past; it is bound in ways that it does not consciously suspect. The psyche is thus always to some degree impaired, for conscious understanding is obstructed by unconscious problems that stand in the way. Only by dealing with these hidden, unresolved conflicts out of the past can the ego deal more effectively with the problems of the present. The quest for a greater range of freedom of action in the present obliges the ego to seek to regain power over its past. That quest is a function of the capacity of the conscious mind to recall the formative experiences of the psyche's life history. To know oneself, therefore, is to retrieve from the oblivion of the unconscious mind lost memories of painful experiences or unresolved conflicts.[7]

Psychoanalysis was the method that Freud invented to oblige the unconscious mind to open its secret history, to reveal to the conscious mind those unrequited desires or unresolved conflicts that unconsciously prompt or paralyze its actions. Such knowledge, once restored to memory, lends power to the ego by enabling it to understand the hidden source of its impairment. In becoming consciously aware of the continuity between past experiences and present perceptions, the ego is strengthened. Knowledge drawn from the unconscious restores to the ego the lost dimensions of its identity. The knowledge of self so derived enhances one's power to cope more realistically with present problems.[8]

The technique of psychoanalysis, therefore, might be likened to an art of memory.[9] It employs a variety of methods for retrieving forgotten memories of past experiences from the unconscious mind: the free association of ideas, the retelling of dreams, the analysis of jokes and of slips of the tongue.[10] Indeed, Freud believed that, barring the organic impairment of the brain, all the memories of our life experience are capable of being recalled from the archive of the unconscious mind.[11] Yet the unconscious mind does not easily give up its secrets, and that is why the role of the analyst is so important. The memories culled from the past through psychoanalytical technique are not transparent representations of past experiences. They are released by the unconscious mind as fragmentary images and must be interpreted if we are to understand the larger pattern from which they are drawn. Sometimes the unconscious mind offers up innocuous substitute, or screen, memories to ward off conscious recognition of forgotten experiences too painful to bear.[12] The analyst's task is

to decode the meaning of the memories recovered. Only with
great skill can he aid his subject in drawing memories forth from
the unconscious mind, and only with great perception can he
correctly interpret their meaning.[13] Successfully conducted,
however, psychoanalysis can reestablish the broken connections
between past and present experiences and so restore to the psyche
the integrity of its identity. Through analysis, the ego becomes
more fully aware of the content of the psyche's life history.
Through such knowledge, the power of the self is asserted.[14]

Though Freud's purpose is therapeutic, he leaves us with the
sense that the psyche is trapped by the contradictions of its own
internal workings.[15] Our destinies are shaped by the drama of
conflicts within our minds. Foucault approaches the problem of the
psyche from the opposite tack. It is not the internal workings of
the mind that initially interested him but the emerging array of
asylums that have fostered scrutiny of the mind over the past
three centuries. All of Foucault's early authorship concerned the
ways in which external authority shapes the structure of the
mind. The historical study of madness that first won him acclaim,
Folie et déraison: Histoire de la folie à l'âge classique (1961), dealt with
the way in which a public definition of sanity/insanity emerged in
the eighteenth century out of the efforts of asylum keepers to
manage nonconformist behavior.[16] His subsequent studies,
Naissance de la clinique (1963)[17] and *Surveiller et punir: Naissance de la
prison* (1975),[18] explored the ramifications of such management, as
behavior that defied public expectations about what was acceptable
was differentiated into a spectrum of types and parceled out
among a variety of institutions—insane asylums, hospitals,
prisons, and other places of segregation. Foucault seeks to show
how the "classical age" (more commonly termed the
Enlightenment) was distinctive not for its faith in intellectual
liberation but rather for its commitment to the disciplining of
human behavior. The asylum was part of a larger institutional
apparatus through which techniques of domination were imposed.
Within these asylums, first the body and then the mind was

subjected to public inspection. In the increasingly nuanced classifications made of the types and limits of normal behavior a public definition of the mind took shape. For this reason, Foucault's early authorship represents an inquiry into the policing function as it is understood in the French sense: the disciplining of human affairs by public and quasi-public agencies.[19]

Foucault's thesis about the policing process is the key to his understanding of the psyche as an abstraction conjured up by public authority to satisfy the need of modern society for a more disciplined conception of the self.[20] It is through the policing process, Foucault contends, that the modern frame of mind has been formed. The policing process fosters a mentality that requires ever more explicit definitions of what is appropriate to human behavior. His studies of asylums are designed to show how over the course of modern history such policing power has spread and intruded into domains of human endeavor previously left untended.[21] In his book on madness, Foucault sought to show that behavior judged merely eccentric in the Middle Ages was deemed embarrassing by the sixteenth century before finally being dismissed as intolerable in the eighteenth century.[22] The notion of sanity, Foucault argues, is a historical definition, imposed by a process ever more relentless in its demands for behavioral conformity. The imperative of the policing process, Foucault explains, is to establish boundaries between regulated and unregulated domains of human activity, which creates a mentality that interprets such activity in terms of binary oppositions: sanity and insanity, health and sickness, legitimate and criminal behavior, lawful and illicit love.[23] Such distinctions, Foucault contends, have been elaborated historically, for human behavior was not previously classified in this way. Only as such behavior becomes subject to public scrutiny does it become necessary to define the boundaries of its legitimacy.

Foucault's thesis about the expanding network of policing powers is somewhat different from Freud's theory of repression. If the accent of the policing process in Freud's interpretation was on constraint, the emphasis for Foucault is on productivity. If certain activities are enjoined by the policing process, Foucault explains, others are engendered by it, so that the elaboration of rules and the rebellion against them are bound together dialectically in spiraling definitions of their relationship to one another.[24] In both his work on insane asylums and that on prisons in the nineteenth century, Foucault shows how the inmates being policed are enticed into participating in, and hence confirming the validity of, the policing process. The madman is encouraged to rid himself of his infirmity by actively seeking a cure.[25] The prisoner is admonished to undertake his own rehabilitation.[26] Both become actors in a ritual designed to confirm the behavioral norms of the society at large. Through this process, Foucault contends, a positive economy of human behavior is delineated. Economy in Foucault's conception of the policing process signifies the production of linguistic and institutional forms through which human beings define their relationships.[27] In this sense, the policing process is the public expression of our essential activity as human beings: the construction of modes of discourse and of action through which we shape our conception of human nature. It is in the formalities of our words and our deeds that we define ourselves. Our human nature is not a hidden reality to be discovered through self-analysis but the aggregate of the forms we have chosen to provide public definitions of who we are.[28] It follows that for Foucault there is no such thing as a human nature. There are only the linguistic and institutional artifacts left behind by successive generations as each took up anew the task of creating categories to explain its perception of the human condition. Since it is the lineage of these discarded systems rather than the meanings they conveyed for generations past that holds Foucault's attention, he likens his method to that of the archaeologist, who also unearths and classifies the relics of the past in terms of their practical uses rather than the abstract values they were intended to affirm.[29]

The forms of classification chosen by each age, moreover,

depend on considerations of power rather than of knowledge.[30] Foucault's interest lies not in the values that successive generations favored but rather in the formalities through which such values were presented. As he traces the implacable spreading of the policing process, he points out the flimsy instability of the arguments advanced to justify it. Although there is continuity in the linguistic and institutional structures designed to carry the policing process forward, the apologies offered for the process shift abruptly over the course of time. The justifications offered for the segregation of deviant behavior, for example, were periodically reconceived from the late Middle Ages to the present, as religious vocabularies were replaced by legal ones, and these in turn by medical and psychological terminologies.[31] The explanations may have changed, Foucault argues, but the process of creating structures with which to measure and contain human behavior have not. Madman and keeper, prisoner and jailer, delinquent and social worker, are all participants in a game whose rules germinate, burgeon, and mature around imperatives of segregation. Eventually, discourse about segregation reaches

beyond the asylum's walls, as public authorities seek to define norms for the society at large in terms of social discipline.[32]

The proposition that there are decisive breaks in the explanations offered for the techniques of policing that public authority employs has become an important hallmark of Foucault's method as a historian.[33] Whereas intellectual historians typically emphasize the continuities in the exchange and dissemination of ideas, Foucault points out the dramatic ruptures in the guiding ideals of Western civilization.[34] The continuities for Foucault are to be found not in the ideals themselves but in the underlying strategies designed to implement them. Indeed, the techniques of policing are sometimes borrowed from one age and reused in the next in unrelated contexts in the name of totally different ideals. For example, madhouses displaced lazar houses between the thirteenth and the eighteenth centuries, but both institutions served as places for the segregation of the group that the society of each of these epochs feared most. As the scrutiny of behavior in the madhouse grew more refined in the early nineteenth century, this asylum was subdivided into a number of more specialized institutions, each with a different theoretical justification. But all of these asylums were part of a policing apparatus in which the imperative to control recalcitrant portions of the population was more important than the therapeutic goals proposed for them.[35]

For Foucault, the policing process operates out of a deep need to mobilize power.[36] Herein his debt to the late-nineteenth-century philosopher, Friedrich Nietzsche, is apparent. Like Nietzsche, Foucault believes that our need to impose structure upon our behavior is derived from a will to power that exists apart from the meanings we employ to justify or explain such authority.[37] The direct correspondence between knowing and doing is denied in the process. In effect, both Foucault and Nietzsche bracket the meanings assigned to human activity in order to trace the connections among the techniques employed to carry them out.[38] Foucault also follows Nietzsche in tracing these connections genealogically rather than historically.[39] As Foucault explains in an essay on Nietzsche, the intellectual historian seeks to account for a theoretical viewpoint by fathoming its intellectual sources. His intent is to return to its earliest conceptualization and then to reconstruct the continuous narrative of the modifications that lead to its present formulation. The genealogist, in contrast, traces patterns of intellectual descent from the present backward without seeking to ascertain their formal beginnings. Since theoretical explanations for courses of action are regarded by Foucault as mere rationalizations, the genealogical descent of our present modes of discourse often springs from unlikely earlier incarnations. In his accent on the erratic and often illogical path of the history of ideas, Foucault, like Nietzsche before him, challenges the notion that there is an intellectual continuity that

Need to understand universe and the place in the world

binds together the history of Western civilization.[40] Foucault is, in the last resort, a wrecker of coherent intellectual systems, one who proceeds not by directly attacking them with opposing arguments but by deconstructing their ancestry with such rigor and in such depth that claims for the pedigree of their intellectual descent are exposed as fraudulent.[41]

Foucault's thesis about the imperative of the policing process to intrude into unregulated domains of human experience also suggests the link between his early work on asylums and his later work on sexuality.[42] His point of departure is the line of demarcation between sexual behavior and open discussion of what is appropriate to it. He focuses on the latter topic, for in his view the more significant revolution in the modern age has been the proliferation of discourse about sexuality. Like madness and criminality, Foucault claims, sex is a topic that, as it has been subjected to public scrutiny, has become bounded by a discussion that seeks to manage it. The sexual revolution of the twentieth century, Foucault believes, has less to do with permissive behavior than it does with a widening discussion of sexuality. The discussion professes to demystify sex in the name of its liberation, yet it is subtly coercive in its classification of techniques of sexual behavior.[43] Such a discussion seeks to police sexuality by publicly defining codes of legitimate and illegitimate sexual behavior. Foucault shows how a discourse initially focused on heterosexuality expanded in the course of the nineteenth century to encompass a wide range of peripheral sexual issues, such as autoeroticism, homosexuality, birth control, and eugenics.[44] Significantly, Foucault emphasizes, the policing of sexuality depends far more on techniques of self-control than did the policing of madness and criminality. For this reason, Foucault's *Histoire de la sexualité*, volume 1, may be viewed as a transitional work from his investigation of the techniques by which external authority manages the mind to the techniques of self-management.[45]

This transition raises the issue of Foucault's conception of the relationship between power and knowledge. In his study of discourse about sexuality, Foucault seeks to show how the inculcation of a discipline of self-control in sexual matters has generated an imperative to seek knowledge of the self. Beginning in seventeenth-century Catholic confessional practices and continuing in twentieth-century psychoanalysis, the task of scrutinizing our sexual behavior came to be understood as a means for better understanding ourselves.[46] Despite the wide differences in their professed purposes, both Catholic confessional technique and Freudian psychoanalytic technique underscore the significance of sexuality in human nature. Because everyone is called upon to monitor his sexual behavior in these modern techniques of self-analysis, knowledge of sexuality and knowledge of ourselves become ever more closely linked. Making sense of our sexuality, Focault holds, is perceived in the modern age to be a method for discovering the truth about who we are. The truth that we seek about ourselves is a truth we associate with the power of self-control. Because the discussion of sexual practices in the modern age has defined sexuality in terms of ever more nuanced boundaries of constraint, the boundaries themselves ironically offer an incitement to transgression in order to discover the hidden meaning of illicit or unexplained sexuality.[47] This desire, together with the heavy burden of self-responsibility imposed on us in our decisions about sexual behavior, has invested the subject with unusual importance in our attempts to understand who we are. Therefore, Foucault concludes, it is not knowledge of our sexuality that gives us power over ourselves (as Freud taught) but our will to establish power over our sexuality that incites our search for self-knowledge.[48]

When Foucault first embarked on his study of sexuality, he anticipated that he would write a six-volume series. Although he completed four volumes before his death in 1984, he had already turned toward a new topic that he had discovered along the way.[49] The study of sexuality had led him to the study of the psyche. It had opened to him a new vista on the nature of the policing process. In his early work on asylums, all of his emphasis had been focused on the technologies of domination employed by public authority in its efforts to manage the mind. His following work on sexuality revealed to him the degree to which technologies of self-management complemented these in furthering the imperatives of the policing process. In his last project on the technologies of the self, all of his attention is focused on the way in which the individual participates in the policing process by monitoring his own behavior.

It is herein that the encounter between Foucault and Freud is directly joined. In his own day, Freud complained of the unwillingness of the French to take seriously his theory of psychoanalysis.[50] If in recent years his doctrine has received a more favorable reception among French scholars, Foucault holds stubbornly to the earlier position—if not to dismiss the psychoanalytic method, at least to challenge the originality of Freud's formulation of it.[51] Freud believed that his psychoanalytic technique was a new invention, made possible by his discovery of the dynamics of the unconscious mind. Foucault, however, wishes to expose its hidden ancestry. He reveals a Freud who, however inventive, borrowed tools of self-analysis with a long genealogy. As he did in tracing the antecedents of modern asylums, Foucault seeks to establish connections between modern psychoanalytic techniques and well-established, if theoretically different, practices of self-analysis in the past. The psychoanalytic method, Foucault contends, is derived from sometimes ancient remedies of self-help, now camouflaged in a medical vocabulary. Although the purposes of self-analysis have changed, he explains, the techniques have not. All of them are devices for enhancing our capacity to assert power over our own behavior. Whereas Freud's accent is on the way in which psychoanalysis enables us to recover lost memories of past experiences, Foucault's concern is with the way in which psychoanalysis appropriates forms of self-help developed and then discarded in earlier times.[52] In this investigation, he remains consistent with the "archaeological" method he developed when he was studying the techniques of domination employed in the management of asylums: He demonstrates how the policing process proliferates apart from the theoretical discussion of its purpose.

The beginnings of Foucault's genealogy of psychoanalysis may be perceived in his earlier discussion of sexuality, in which he points out the way in which Freud appropriated the techniques of auricular confession of the Catholic church and thereby clothed the examination of conscience, a religious practice, in a medical garb.[53] But in his later studies on the shaping of the psyche, Foucault shows how these technologies of the self have a still earlier ancestry. Just as Freud sought to trace the structural formation of the psyche to primal events at the beginning of human civilization, so Foucault in this last line of inquiry proceeds deeper into the past than he had in any of his earlier studies. He retraces the lineage of seventeenth-century confessional practices to the Christian Roman Empire of the fourth and fifth centuries, specifically to the prescribed routines of monastic life. In that context, Foucault explains, penance was not simply a confessional act but a long-term status with diverse penitential obligations: mortification of the flesh, contemplation to rid oneself of earthly desires, absolute obedience to one's spiritual director, and the examination of conscience as a prelude to public confession at the end of the period of penance. Knowledge of the self, these spiritual directors taught, was derived from its chastening.[54]

But even these rituals for self-examination, Foucault continues, are derived from still earlier practices. Many of these techniques predate Christian practice. Some were borrowed from the Stoics, who had developed an elaborate regimen of self-discipline in the first and second centuries A.D. to further a different, purely humanistic notion of self-analysis. Practices such as the spiritual retreat, meditation, ritual purification, and deference to a mentor,

all subsequently employed by Christian spiritual directors, had
been used by Stoic teachers for quite different purposes. Though
suspect among many Stoics, the interpretation of dreams was also
a highly popular technique of self-care in antiquity, for dreams
were believed to be portents of the future for which it was
important to prepare.[55] The Stoic ideal was not self-denial, as it
would be for later Christians, but rather self-care. Stoic
techniques were designed to enable one to cope with the realities
of this world more effectively, not to prepare for a spiritual world
beyond.[56] But even the practices for self-care of the Stoics had
earlier precedents. The Pythagoreans of the fifth and fourth
centuries B.C. instructed their initiates in the virtues of an ordered
life and obliged them to observe silence and to learn the art of
listening as a route to self-mastery. During the same era,
Plato, in his dialogue *Alcibiades I*, presents Socrates teaching his
young disciple a method for self-care as a means of preparing him
for the adult responsibilities of public life.[57]

Because Foucault terminates his genealogical probe into the
techniques of self-analysis at this juncture, one might be tempted
to treat these Pythagorean and Platonic methods as the founding
precedents for the development of the technologies of the self in
the ancient world. But Foucault implies that the descent of these
practices could be traced back even further. His point is that
there is no starting point, as Freud supposed there was, but only
a genealogical chain to earlier formulations that disappear
eventually into the oblivion of prehistory.[58] Humankind's point of
departure for self-understanding, Foucault contends, begins
today, not in some hypothetical beginning of historical time. Each
day we make ourselves anew in fresh formulations. By
deconstructing this genealogical descent into the past, Foucault
seeks to expose the methods of Freudian psychoanalysis as the
tools of forgotten philosophies of the self, honed by the analysts
of earlier epochs who hailed from different intellectual traditions
and who had unrelated purposes in mind. The Freud who
descends from the genealogy of psychoanalysis in Foucault's

deconstruction is not the creator of a new method but an inventor whose genius it was to bring together into a unified theory of medical discourse the techniques of self-analysis used and then discarded by the past societies of Western civilization. Like the therapists of our own society, these earlier practitioners regarded the care of the self as a serious and salutary pursuit, even if they expressed their commitment to it in an ethical or religious rather than a medical vocabulary. The question that Foucault asks of Freud is why he seeks to discover the truth about the self through these techniques, whereas his predecessors had been content to search for a method of self-care.[59]

Freud's answer to that question, of course, was bound up with a quite different perception of what we can know about the psyche. Whatever the interpretative limits of language, Freud would counter, the psyche is a discrete reality whose workings we can objectively understand.[60] Our conception of the psyche may be limited by the images we employ to describe it. But the inadequacy of our theory does not diminish the reality of the object it seeks to define. The task is to refine our theory so that we may approach the truth about the psyche's nature more closely. Foucault, on the other hand, argues that the self is not an objective reality to be described by our theories but a subjective notion that is actually constituted by them. The self is an abstract construction, one continually being redesigned in an ongoing discourse generated by the imperatives of the policing process. In tracing the genealogy of this discourse, Foucault contends, we discover that the self is no more than a congeries of theories about its nature. Theories of the self are a kind of currency through which power over the mind is defined and extended. Foucault, therefore, inverts Freud's proposition about the relationship between knowledge and power. Whereas Freud sought to explain how knowledge gives us power over the self, Foucault seeks to demonstrate how power shapes our knowledge of the self.

This fundamental difference in approach becomes apparent if we compare Freud's and Foucault's views on the topic of sexuality. Because sex was a topic about which there was little public discussion at the turn of the twentieth century, Freud's task was to overcome his contemporaries' reluctance to acknowledge sex as a major source of human motivation.[61] For Freud, the discussion of sexuality was an important avenue to intellectual enlightenment. To a large degree, he contended, the truth about our human nature is grounded in our sexuality, for sexual energy (libido) is the matrix of human creativity. Its energy is stored by the unconscious psyche and is transformed as it is sublimated in cultural endeavor.[62] By discovering the power of sexual impulses to motivate all manner of human behavior not consciously perceived to be sexual, we learn a previously hidden truth about ourselves that is liberating. Foucault, by contrast, writes in an age in which the discussion of sex seems to him to be less liberating than constraining in the degree of scrutiny to which sex has been subjected and in the depth of public surveillance such scrutiny implies. His interest, therefore, is in the way our growing sense of obligation to talk about sex as a means of understanding our human nature has made discourse about sexuality a contemporary frontier of the policing process.[63]

This distinction between discourse about sexuality as a source of self-knowledge and as an arena for the display of power over the self points to more far-reaching differences between these two philosophers. Freud is chiefly concerned with origins. He insists on the determining power of experience as a precedent for future behavior. Such precedents are compelling in the formation of both our personal and our collective identity.[64] The experiences of the past have indelibly etched the surfaces of our psyches, providing the fundamental designs of behavior with which we will henceforth live. Present actions are always undertaken in light of unconscious memories of such experiences. But if human nature for Freud is shaped by the recollection of past experience, it is for Foucault constructed through humankind's activity as a maker of forms. Indeed, for Foucault, past experiences are lost in the maze of formulas humans have created to classify them. Foucault argues that we discover our identity not by fathoming the original meaning of behavior precedents, as Freud taught, but rather by deconstructing the formalities through which we endlessly examine, evaluate, and classify our experiences. If Freud glances back to original experience as it points toward the future, Foucault's gaze remains fixed on the present. Whereas Freud asks how our past experience shapes our lives in the present, Foucault asks why we seek to discover truth in the formal rules that we have designed to discipline life's experiences. Freud's concern about the past emphasizes recollection. Foucault, in contrast, stresses repetition, which reinforces his central proposition about the paradox of the human condition: We are beings that create forms which ironically imprison our creativity. This pattern of creation and constraint is ceaselessly repeated. Past experiences, Foucault argues, do not shape us irrevocably, as Freud believed. Rather, we continually reshape our past creations to conform to our present creative needs.

The question of parenting provides a good example of this distinction between their approaches to the formation of self-identity. Freud stresses inheritance. For him, the role of the parent, both immediately and primordially, is all-important. To understand ourselves, he argues, we investigate our relationships to our parents to ascertain how these have shaped the deep structures of our unconscious minds. The connections are real, even if they have been repressed and forgotten. Correspondingly, our earliest ancestors have bequeathed to us institutional precedents for dealing with our experiences, and these continue to influence us in profound ways. Freud, for example, was in awe of the tenacious power of appeal of religion, so deeply was it embedded in the collective memory of humankind. Freud's return to origins in his search for both our individual and our collective identities was based on his faith in the enduring power of precedent to determine our present behavior.[65]

Foucault, in contrast, traces genealogical descent from the present backward. For him, parentage is not determining but accidental. One need only reconstruct his genealogy a few generations into the near past to see the random, fortuitous, and sometimes bizarre course of his own descent. If one seeks to return to origins, as did Freud, one hopes to uncover the continuity between one's heritage and one's present aspirations. But if one reverses the process and traces one's ancestry, Foucault explains, one will encounter striking discontinuities. Just as children sometimes live markedly different lives from those of their parents, so the use of ideas by one generation may bear little relationship to those of the preceding one.[66] This suggests why Foucault attaches so little importance to ideas in and of themselves in any given age, for he has no faith in the formative power of intellectual tradition.[67]

Finally, the difference between these two philosophers is revealed in their respective conceptions of the technologies of the self. Herein they consider the problem of the cultural significance of memory. Freud's preeminent concern is self-knowledge. He believes that the techniques of psychoanalysis enable us to dredge forgotten experiences from the bottom of the unconscious mind and to bring them to the surface of conscious understanding. To know oneself is to return to these origins of experience. Obliging the unconscious to return to the conscious mind its concealed memories of our past experiences is liberating, for therein we discover the forgotten influences that have made us what we are. The memories recalled reestablish our sense of continuity with the past and hence show us the truth about ourselves. Freud's theory of the self, therefore, underscores the historical significance of memory as the foundation of identity. In reaching back to origins to recollect lost fragments of our experience, memory makes us whole once more by reaffirming our connection with the past.[68]

Freud's faith was that all forgotten experiences are retrievable from a reservoir of repressed memories that await recollection. It is a reassuring faith in the age of intellectual fragmentation in which we live. If there is little coherence in our present

philosophies, there is at least a unity of meaning to be discer
in the continuity of our life experience, stored in the archive of
the unconscious mind. When we consciously reconstruct that
experience we are reassured about who we are.[69] Although
Foucault would concede that Freud's psychoanalytic method
discloses significant meanings about ourselves, he would contend
that none of these can provide us with a definitive understanding.
The search for the self is a journey into a mental labyrinth that
takes random courses and ultimately ends at impasses. The
memory fragments recovered along the way cannot provide us
with a basis for interpreting the overall meaning of the journey.
The meanings that we derive from our memories are only partial
truths, and their value is ephemeral.[70] For Foucault, the psyche is
not an archive but only a mirror. To search the psyche for the
truth about ourselves is a futile task because the psyche can only
reflect the images we have conjured up to describe ourselves.
Looking into the psyche, therefore, is like looking into the mirror
image of a mirror. One sees oneself reflected in an image of infinite
regress. Our gaze is led not toward the substance of our
beginnings but rather into the meaninglessness of previously
discarded images of the self. In the end, the meaning of the self
for Foucault is less important than the methods we employ to
understand it. It is in the technologies of the self that humans
have employed across the centuries that we find continuities. What
we seek in psychoanalysis is what the Christian confessors and the
Stoics sought long ago—not self-knowledge but a method of self-
care.

Does Foucault's argument about the discontinuities in the
meanings to be derived from our past experiences condemn us to
personal and cultural amnesia? Foucault's purpose is not to deny
the value and importance of recalling the past but to change our
perspective on that endeavor. What fathoming the past teaches us
is that there are options among which we are free to choose, not
simply continuities to which we must adapt. Who we are has as

much to do with what we affirm in the present as it does with what we revere in the past. The quest for self-understanding is a journey without end. Even in the deepest recesses of our psyches there are no experiences which, if evoked, will reveal our true identities. But the quest for such knowledge is itself a form of self-care, as ancient practitioners of the technologies of the self taught long before Freud. Therefore, Foucault contends, we are condemned to a quest for meaning whose meaning is that our human nature is continually being reconstituted by the forms that we create along the way. The responsibility to create meanings and values anew is a perpetual task but nonetheless the foundation of all human endeavor. For Foucault, it is through such creativity that our power is revealed, and it is in our capacity to use it well that our destiny lies.

Notes

1   See esp. Michel Foucault, "Nietzsche, Freud, Marx," *Cahiers de Royaumont: Philosophie* 6 (1967): 183–92; *The Order of Things: An Archaeology of the Human Sciences* (New York: Pantheon, 1970), pp. 373–81; *Madness and Civilization: A History of Insanity in the Age of Reason* (New York: Pantheon, 1965), pp. 277–78; "The Confession of the Flesh," in *Power/Knowledge: Selected Interviews and Other Writings, 1972–1977*, ed. Colin Gordon (New York: Pantheon, 1980), pp. 211–13.

2   For the relationship between Foucault's historical studies and recent work in the history of collective mentalities, see Patrick H. Hutton, "The History of Mentalities: The New Map of Cultural History," *History and Theory* 20, no. 3 (1981): 237–59.

3   On Freud in historical context, see esp. Lancelot Law Whyte, *The Unconscious before Freud* (New York: Basic Books, 1960), pp. x, 10, 75, 169, 177–81; Henri F. Ellenberger, *The Discovery of the Unconscious: The History and Evolution of Dynamic Psychiatry* (New York: Basic Books, 1970), pp. 480, 488–89, 492–93, 514, 516, 534–46; Arthur K. Berliner, *Psychoanalysis and Society: The Social Thought of Sigmund Freud* (Washington, D.C.: University Press of America, 1983), pp. 13–25.

4   Sigmund Freud, *An Outline of Psychoanalysis*, trans. James Strachey (New York: Norton, 1949), pp. 13–18.

5   Ibid., p. 32; Sigmund Freud, *Leonardo da Vinci: A Study in Psychosexuality*,

trans. A. A. Brill (New York: Vintage Books, 1947), p. 121.

6   Sigmund Freud, *Civilization and Its Discontents*, trans. James Strachey (New York: Norton, 1961), pp. 23–30.

7   Freud, *Outline of Psychoanalysis*, pp. 63, 70.

8   Ibid., pp. 61–79.

9   On the relationship between Freud's psychoanalytic method and classic mnemonic technique, see Patrick H. Hutton, "The Art of Memory Reconceived: From Rhetoric to Psychoanalysis," *Journal of the History of Ideas* 48, no. 3 (1987).

10   Freud, *Outline of Psychoanalysis*, p. 71; *The Psychopathology of Everyday Life*, trans. Alan Tyson (New York: Norton, 1965).

11   Sigmund Freud, *The Interpretation of Dreams*, trans. James Strachey (New York: Avon Books, 1965), p. 54.

12   Sigmund Freud, "Screen Memories," in *The Standard Edition of the Complete Psychological Works of Sigmund Freud*, trans. and ed. James Strachey (London, 1962), 3:303–22; *Psychopathology of Everyday Life*, pp. 43–52.

13   Freud, *Interpretation of Dreams*, pp. 44–55.

14   Freud, *Outline of Psychoanalysis*, pp. 70, 77.

15   Ibid., pp. 103–23; Freud, *Civilization and Its Discontents*, pp. 71–80, 86–89.

16   Trans. as *Madness and Civilization*.

17   Trans. as *The Birth of the Clinic: An Archaeology of Medical Perception*, by A. M. Sheridan-Smith (New York: Pantheon, 1973).

18   Trans. as *Discipline and Punish: The Birth of the Prison* by Alan Sheridan (New York: Pantheon, 1977).

19   Michel Foucault, "The Politics of Health in the Eighteenth Century," in *Power/Knowledge*, pp. 170–71; *Omnes et Singulatim*: Towards a Criticism of 'Political Reason,' " in *The Tanner Lectures on Human Values*, ed. Sterling M. McMurrin (Salt Lake City: University of Utah Press, 1981), 2:246–54; cf. Jacques Donzelot, *The Policing of Families*, trans. Robert Hurley (New York: Pantheon, 1979), pp. 6–7; Foucault, "The Political Technology of Individuals" (Chapter 8, herein).

20   Foucault, "*Omnes et Singulatim*," pp. 237–40; "The Political Technology of Individuals," herein.

21   Foucault, "*Omnes et Singulatim*, pp. 226–27.

22   Foucault, "*Madness and Civilization*, pp. 3–64.

23   "The History of Sexuality: An Interview with Michel Foucault," in *Power/Knowledge*, p. 185.

24   Michel Foucault, "Truth and Power," in *Power/Knowledge*, pp. 109–33.

25   Foucault, *Madness and Civilization*, pp. 246–55.

26   Foucault, *Discipline and Punish*, pp. 231–48.

27   Michel Foucault, "Two Lectures" and "The Eye of Power," in *Power/Knowledge*, pp. 88–92, 158–65; cf. Charles C. Lemert and Garth Gillan,

Michel Foucault: Social Theory as Transgression (New York: Columbia University Press, 1982), pp. 76–77, 111–12.

28 Foucault, *The Order of Things*, pp. xx–xxii, 368–69.

29 Michel Foucault, *The Archaeology of Knowledge*, trans. A. M. Sheridan Smith (New York: Harper, 1976), pp. 7, 131, 138–40, 147; cf. Allan Megill, *Prophets of Extremity* (Berkeley: University of California Press, 1985), pp. 227–32.

30 Foucault, "Prison Talk" and "Truth and Power," in *Power/Knowledge*, pp. 51–52, 112–14.

31 Foucault, *Madness and Civilization*, pp. 35, 63–64, 221–24, 250–51; *Discipline and Punish*, pp. 298–308.

32 Foucault, *Discipline and Punish*, pp. 298–308.

33 For discussions of Foucault's argument about decisive breaks between discrete cultural epochs (which he terms "epistemes"), see Jean Piaget, *Structuralism*, trans. Chaninah Maschler (New York: Harper, 1971), pp. 131–35; Hayden V. White, "Foucault Decoded: Notes from the Underground," *History and Theory* 12 (1975): 27–28; Allan Megill, "Foucault, Structuralism, and the Ends of History," *Journal of Modern History* 51 (1951): 462–66; Lemert and Gillan, *Foucault*, pp. 7–14.

34 Foucault, *The Order of Things*, pp. xxii, 217, 250, 367; *The Archaeology of Knowledge*, pp. 3–17; "History of Sexuality," in *Power/Knowledge*, p. 185.

35 Foucault, *Madness and Civilization*, pp. 38–64, 241–78; *Discipline and Punish*, pp. 73–103.

36 Foucault, "*Omnes et Singulatim*," pp. 253–54.

37 Michel Foucault, "Nietzsche, Genealogy, History," in *Language, Counter-memory, Practice: Selected Essays and Interviews*, ed. Donald F. Bouchard (Ithaca, N.Y.: Cornell University Press, 1977), pp. 148–52.

38 Ibid., pp. 142, 151–52.

39 Foucault, "Two Lectures," p. 83.

40 Foucault, "Nietzsche, Genealogy, History," pp. 139–64; cf. Pamela Major-Poetzl, *Michel Foucault's Archaeology of Western Culture: Toward a New Science of History* (Chapel Hill: University of North Carolina Press, 1983), pp. 36–42.

41 Foucault, *Madness and Civilization*, pp. 279–89.

42 Michel Foucault, *The History of Sexuality: An Introduction*, trans. Robert Hurley (New York: Pantheon, 1978), 1:10–13.

43 Ibid., pp. 92–102, 115–31; "History of Sexuality," in *Power/Knowledge*, pp. 190–91.

44 Foucault, *History of Sexuality*, 1:69–70, 77–80; "History of Sexuality," in *Power/Knowledge*, pp. 191–92.

45   "History of Sexuality," in *Power/Knowledge*, pp. 181–89.

46   Foucault, *History of Sexuality*, 1:53–70, 77–80; "History of Sexuality," in *Power/Knowledge*, pp. 191–92.

47   Foucault, *History of Sexuality*, 1:113; cf. Karlis Racevskis, *Michel Foucault and the Subversion of the Intellect* (Ithaca, N.Y.: Cornell University Press, 1983), p. 110.

48   Foucault, *History of Sexuality*, 1:77–80, 92, 129–31, 155–59.

49   "On the Genealogy of Ethics: An Overview of Work in Progress—An Interview with Michel Foucault," in *The Foucault Reader*, ed. Paul Rabinow (New York: Pantheon, 1984), pp. 340–43.

50   Sigmund Freud, *An Autobiographical Study*, trans. James Strachey (New York: Norton, 1952), pp. 21, 118–19.

51   André Burguière, "The Fate of the History of Mentalities in the *Annales*," *Comparative Studies in Society and History* 24, no. 3 (1982): 424–37; Mark Poster, *Foucault, Marxism, and History* (Cambridge: Polity, 1984), pp. 32–34; Sherry Turkle, *Psychoanalytic Politics: Freud's French Revolution* (New York: Basic Books, 1978), pp. 27–68.

52   Foucault, *History of Sexuality*, 1:112–13, 129–31; "History of Sexuality," in *Power/Knowledge*, pp. 191–92.

53   Foucault, *History of Sexuality*, 1:18–24, 58–65, 67, 112–13, 119, 130.

54   Michel Foucault, "Technologies of the Self" (chapter 2, herein).

55   Foucault, "Technologies of the Self," herein; see also Luther H. Martin, "Artemidorus: Dream Theory in Late Antiquity," *Second Century* (forthcoming).

56   Foucault, "Technologies of the Self," herein; *Histoire de la sexualité, vol. 3, le souci de soi* (Paris: Gallimard, 1984), pp. 59–69, 75–85; "Genealogy of Ethics," in *Foucault Reader*, pp. 342, 359–62.

57   Foucault, "Technologies of the Self," herein. *Histoire de la sexualité*, 3:58–59, 65, 77.

58   Foucault, *The Order of Things*, pp. 328–35; "Nietzsche, Genealogy, History," in *Language*, pp. 142–47.

59   Foucault, "Technologies of the Self," herein.

60   Sigmund Freud, *New Introductory Lectures on Psychoanalysis*, trans. James Strachey (New York: Norton, 1965), pp. 170, 175–76, 181–82; *Outline of Psychoanalysis*, pp. 40, 105.

61   J. N. Isbister, *Freud: An Introduction to His Life and Work* (Cambridge: Polity, 1985), pp. 69, 83; Richard Wollheim, *Sigmund Freud* (New York: Viking Press, 1971), pp. 113–18.

62   Freud, "Three Essays on the Theory of Sexuality," in *Standard Edition of Freud*, 7:231–43; *Autobiographical Study*, pp. 6–73; *Outline of Psychoanalysis*, p. 114; *Civilization and Its Discontents*, p. 44.

63   Foucault, *History of Sexuality*, 1:23–25, 69–70.

64   Freud, *Leonardo da Vinci*, pp. 31, 37, 72–73, 94–98, 104–7, 110–22; *Moses and Monotheism*, trans. Katherine Jones (New York: Vintage Books, 1967), pp. 144–47, 160–64.

65   Freud, *Moses and Monotheism*, pp. 131–76; *Civilization and Its Discontents*, pp. 11–22; *The Future of an Illusion*, trans. James Strachey (New York: Norton, 1961), pp. 42–50.

66   Foucault, "Two Lectures," in *Power/Knowledge*, pp. 83–84, 87; "Nietzsche, Genealogy, History," in *Language*, pp. 142–47.

67   Foucault, *Archaeology of Knowledge*, pp. 135–40.

68   Freud, *Moses and Monotheism*, pp. 164–69.

69   Freud, *Interpretation of Dreams*, p. 54.

70   Foucault, "Nietzsche, Genealogy, History," in *Language*, pp. 142–47, 160–64.

Eight THE POLITICAL TECHNOLOGY

OF INDIVIDUALS

MICHEL FOUCAULT

The general framework of what I call the "Technologies of the Self" is a question which appeared at the end of the eighteenth century. It was to become one of the poles of modern philosophy. This question is very different from what we call the traditional philosophical questions: What is the world? What is man? What is truth? What is knowledge? How can we know something? And so on. The question, I think, which arises at the end of the eighteenth century is: What are we in our actuality? You will find the formulation of this question in a text written by Kant. I don't pretend that the previous questions about truth, knowledge, and so on have to be put aside. On the contrary, they constitute a very strong and consistent field of analysis, what I would like to call the formal ontology of truth. But I think that a new pole has been constituted for the activity of philosophizing, and this pole is characterized by the question, the permanent and ever-changing question, "What are we today?" And that is, I think, the field of the historical reflection on ourselves. Kant, Fichte, Hegel, Nietzsche, Max Weber, Husserl, Heidegger, the *Frankfurterschule*, have tried to answer this question. What I am trying to do, referring to this tradition, is to give very partial and provisory

Portions of this chapter were previously published in *The Tanner Lectures on Human Values*, vol. 2, as "Omnes et Singulatim." Permission to use this material has been granted by University of Utah Press (© 1981).

answers to this question through the history of thought or, more precisely, through the historical analysis of the relationships between our thought and our practices in Western society.

Let's say very briefly that through studying madness and psychiatry, crime and punishment, I have tried to show how we have indirectly constituted ourselves through the exclusion of some others: criminals, mad people, and so on. And now my present work deals with the question: How did we directly constitute our identity through some ethical techniques of the self which developed through antiquity down to now? That was what we were studying in the seminar.

There now is another field of questions that I would like to study: the way by which, through some political technology of individuals, we have been led to recognize ourselves as a society, as a part of a social entity, as a part of a nation or of a state. I would like now to give you an *aperçu*, not of the technologies of the self but of the political technology of individuals.

Of course, I am afraid that the material I have to deal with could be a little too technical and historical for a so-called public lecture. I am not a public lecturer, and I know this material would be much more convenient for a seminar. But I have two good reasons to present it to you in spite of the fact it may be too technical. First, I think it is always a little pretentious to present in a more or less prophetic way what people have to think. I prefer to let them draw their own conclusions or infer general ideas from the interrogations I try to raise in analyzing historical and specific material. I think it's much more respectful for everyone's freedom, and that's my manner. The second reason why I will present rather technical materials to you is that I don't know why people in a public lecture would be less clever, less smart, or less well read than in a classroom. Let us then begin with this problem of the political technology of individuals.

In 1779, the first volume of a book entitled *System einer vollstaendigen Medicinische Polizei* by the German author J. P. Frank was brought out, to be followed by five other tomes. And when the last volume was published in 1790, the French Revolution had already begun. Why do I bring together this celebrated event of the French Revolution and this obscure book? The reason is simple. Frank's work is the first great systematic program of public health for the modern state. It indicates with a lot of detail what an administration has to do to insure the wholesome food, good housing, health care, and medical institutions which the population needs to remain healthy, in short, to foster the life of individuals. Through this book we can see that the care for individual life is becoming at this moment a duty for the state.

At the same moment the French Revolution gives the signal for the great national wars of our days, involving national armies and meeting their conclusion or their climax in huge mass slaughters. I think that you can see a similar phenomenon during the Second World War. In all history it would be hard to find such butchery as in World War II, and it is precisely this period, this moment, when the great welfare, public health, and medical assistance programs were instigated. The Beveridge program has been, if not conceived, at least published at this very moment. One could symbolize such a coincidence by a slogan: Go get slaughtered and we promise you a long and pleasant life. Life insurance is connected with a death command.

The coexistence in political structures or large destructive mechanisms and institutions oriented toward the care of individual life is something puzzling and needs some investigation. It is one of the central antinomies of our political reason. It is this antinomy of our political rationality which I'd like to consider. I don't mean that mass slaughters are the effect, the result, the logical consequence of our rationality, nor do I mean that the state has the obligation of taking care of individuals since it has the right to kill millions of people. Neither do I want to deny that mass slaughters or social care have their economic explanations or their emotional motivations.

Excuse me if I go back to the same point: We are thinking beings. That means that even when we kill or when we are killed, even when we make war or when we ask for support as unemployed, even when we vote for or against a government which cuts social security expenses and increases defense spending, even in these cases, we are thinking beings, and we do these things not only on the ground of universal rules of behavior but also on the specific ground of a historical rationality. It is this rationality, and the death and life game which takes place in it, that I'd like to investigate from a historical point of view. This type of rationality, which is one of the main features of the modern political rationality, developed in the seventeenth and eighteenth centuries through the general idea of the "reason of state" and also through a very specific set of techniques of government which were called at this moment, and with a very special meaning, the police.

Let's begin with the "reason of state." I'll recall briefly a few definitions borrowed from Italian and German authors. An Italian jurist, Botero, at the end of the sixteenth century, gives this definition of the reason of state: "A perfect knowledge of the means through which states form, strengthen themselves, endure and grow." Another Italian author, Palazzo, writes in the beginning of the seventeenth century [*Discourse on Government and True Reason of State*, 1606]: "A reason of state is a rule or an art enabling us to discover how to establish peace and order within the republic." And Chemnitz, a German author in the middle of the seventeenth century [*De Ratione Status*, 1647], gives this definition: "A certain political consideration required for all public matters, councils, and projects, whose only aim is the state's preservation, expansion, and felicity"— note those words: the state's preservation, the state's expansion, and the state's felicity—"to which end, the easiest and the promptest means are to be employed."

Let's consider certain features those definitions have in

common. Reason of state, first, is regarded as an "art," that is, as a technique conforming to certain rules. These rules pertain not simply to customs and traditions but to a certain rational knowledge. Nowadays, the expression "reason of state," as you know, evokes much more arbitrariness or violence. But, at the time, what people had in mind was a rationality specific to the art of governing states. From where does this specific art of government draw its rationale? The answer to this question, provoked at the beginning of the seventeenth century, is the scandal of the nascent political thought, and yet the answer, following the authors I have quoted, was very simple. The art of governing people is rational on the condition that it observes the nature of what is governed, that is, the state itself.

Now, to formulate such an evidence, such a platitude, was in fact to break simultaneously with two opposite traditions: the Christian tradition and Machiavelli's theory. The Christian tradition claimed that if government was to be essentially just, it had to respect a whole system of laws: human, natural, and divine.

There is a significant text written by Saint Thomas on this point, where he explains that the king's government must imitate God's government of nature: The king must found cities just as God has created the world; he must lead man toward his finality just as God does for natural beings. And what is man's finality? Is it physical health? No, answers Saint Thomas. If physical health were the finality of man, then we would need not a king but a physician. Is it wealth? No, because in this case a steward and not a king would suffice. Is is truth? No, answers Saint Thomas, because to attain truth we don't need a king, we need only a teacher. Man needs someone capable of opening up the way to heavenly bliss through his conformity on earth to what is *honestum*. A king has to lead man toward *honestum* as his natural and divine finality.

Saint Thomas's model for rational government is not at all a political one, whereas in the sixteenth and seventeenth centuries people are seeking for other denominations of reason of state, principles capable of guiding an actual government. They are concerned with what the state is and not with the divine or the natural finalities of man.

Reason of state is also opposed to another kind of analysis. In *The Prince*, Machiavelli's problem is to decide how a province or a territory acquired through inheritance or by conquest can be held against its internal and external rivals. Machiavelli's entire analysis is aimed at defining what reinforces the link between prince and state, whereas the problem posed in the beginning of the seventeenth century by the notion of reason of state is that of the very existence and nature of this new entity which is the state itself. The theoreticians of reason of state tried to keep aloof from Machiavelli both because he had at this moment a very bad reputation and because they couldn't recognize their own problem in his problem, which was not the problem of the state but the problem of the relationships between the prince—the king—and his territory and his people. Despite all the quarrels about the prince and Machiavelli's work, reason of state is a milestone in the emergence of an extremely different type of rationality from that of the conception of Machiavelli. The aim of this new art of governing is precisely not to reinforce the power of the prince. Its aim is to reinforce the state itself.

In a few words, reason of state refers neither to the wisdom of God nor to the reason or the strategies of the prince. It refers to the state, to its nature, and to its own rationality. This thesis that the aim of a government is to strengthen the state itself implies several ideas which I think are important to touch upon to follow the rise and development of our modern political rationality.

The first of those ideas is the new relation between politics as a practice and as knowledge. It concerns the possibility of a specific political knowledge. Following Saint Thomas, the king had only to be virtuous. The leader of the city in the Platonic republic had to be a philosopher. For the first time, the one who has to rule others in the framework of the state has to be a politician, has to attain a specific political competence and knowledge.

The state is something which exists per se. It is a kind of natural object, even if the jurists try to know how it can be constituted in a legitimate way. The state is by itself an order of things, and political knowledge separates it from juridical reflections. Political knowledge deals not with the rights of people or with human or divine laws but with the nature of the state which has to be governed. Government is possible only when the strength of the state is known: It is by this knowledge that it can be sustained. The state's capacity and the means to enlarge it must be known. The strength and the capacity of other states, rivals of my own state, must also be known. The governed state must hold out against the others. A government, therefore, entails more than just implementing general principles of reason, wisdom, and prudence. A certain specific knowledge is necessary: concrete, precise, and measured knowledge as to the state's strength. The art of governing characteristic of the reason of state is intimately bound up with the development of what was called, at this moment, political arithmetic. Political arithmetic was the knowledge implied by political competence, and you know very well that the other name of this political arithmetic was statistics, a statistics related not at all to probability but to the knowledge of state, the knowledge of different states' respective forces.

The second important point derived from this idea of reason of state is the rise of new relationships between politics and history. The true nature of the state in this perspective is not conceived anymore as an equilibrium between several elements that only a good law could bring and maintain together. It is conceived as a set of forces and strengths that could be increased or weakened according to the politics followed by the governments. These forces have to be increased since each state is in a permanent competition with other countries, other nations, and other states, so that each state has nothing before it other than an indefinite future of struggles, or at least of competitions, with similar states. The idea which had been predominant throughout the Middle Ages was that all the kingdoms on the earth would be one day unified in one last empire just before the Christ's return to earth. From the beginning of the seventeenth century, this familiar idea is nothing more than a dream, which was also one of the main features of political thought, or of historical-political thought, during the Middle Ages. This project of reconstituting the Roman Empire vanishes forever. Politics has now to deal with an irreducible multiplicity of states struggling and competing in a limited history.

The third idea we can derive from this notion of reason of state is this: Since the state is its own finality and since the governments must have for an exclusive aim not only the conservation but also the permanent reinforcement and development of the state's strengths, it is clear that the governments don't have to worry about individuals; or government has to worry about them only insofar as they are somehow relevant for the reinforcement of the state's strength: what they do, their life, their death, their activity, their individual behavior, their work, and so on. I would say that in this kind of analysis of the relationships between the individual and the state, the individual becomes pertinent for the state insofar as he can do something for the strength of the state. But there is in this perspective something which we could call a kind of political marginalism, since what is in question here is only political utility. From the state's point of view, the individual exists insofar as what he does is able to introduce even a minimal change in the strength of the state, either in a positive or in a negative direction. It is only insofar as an individual is able to introduce this change that the state has to do with him. And sometimes what he has to do for the state is to live, to work, to produce, to consume; and sometimes what he has to do is to die.

Apparently those ideas are similar to a lot of ideas we can find

in Greek philosophy. And, indeed, reference to Greek cities is
very current in this political literature of the beginning of the
seventeenth century. But I think that under a few similar themes
something quite different is going on in this new political theory.
The marginalistic integration of individuals in the state's utility is
not obtained in the modern state by the form of the ethical
community which was characteristic of the Greek city. It is
obtained in this new political rationality by a certain specific
technique called then, and at this moment, the police.

Here we meet the problem I would like to analyze in some
future work. The problem is this: Which kind of political
techniques, which technology of government, has been put to
work and used and developed in the general framework of the
reason of state in order to make of the individual a significant
element for the state? Most of the time, when one analyzes the
role of the state in our society, either one focuses attention on
institutions—armies, civil service, bureaucracy, and so on—and
on the kind of people who rule them, or one analyzes the theories
or the ideologies which were developed in order to justify or to
legitimate the existence of the state.

What I am looking for, on the contrary, are the techniques, the
practices, which give a concrete form to this new political
rationality and to this new kind of relationship between the social
entity and the individual. And, surprisingly enough, people, at
least in countries like Germany and France, where for different
reasons the problem of state was considered as a major issue,
recognized the necessity of defining, describing, and organizing
very explicitly this new technology of power, the new techniques
by which the individual could be integrated into the social entity.
They recognized its necessity, and they gave it a name. This
name in French is *police*, and in German, *Polizei*. (I think the
meaning of the English word, police, is something very different.)
We must precisely try to give better definitions of what was
understood by those French and German words, *police* and *Polizei*.

The meaning of these German and French words is puzzling

since they have been used at least from the nineteenth century until now to designate something else, a very specific institution which at least in France and Germany—I don't know about the United States—didn't always have a very good reputation. But, from the end of the sixteenth century to the end of the eighteenth century, the words *police* and *Polizei* had a very broad and, at the same time, also a very precise meaning. When people spoke about police at this moment, they spoke about the specific techniques by which a government in the framework of the state was able to govern people as individuals significantly useful for the world.

In order to analyze a little more precisely this new technology of government, I think that it is best to catch it in the three major forms that any technology is able to take in its development and its history: as a dream or, better, as a utopia; then as a practice or as rules for some real institutions; and then as an academic discipline.

Louis Turquet de Mayenne provides a good example at the beginning of the seventeenth century of contemporary opinion concerning the utopian or universal technique of government. His book, *La Monarchie aristo-démocratique* (1611), proposed the specialization of executive power and of police powers. The task of the police was to foster civil respect and public morality.

Turquet proposed that there should be in each province four boards of police to keep law and order, two of which see to the people and two others which had to see to things. The first board was to look after the positive, active, productive aspects of life. In other words, this board was concerned with education, with determining very precisely each individual's aptitudes and tastes. It had to test the aptitude of the children from the very beginning of their lives. Each person over the age of twenty-five had to be enrolled on a register noting his aptitudes and his occupation; the rest were regarded as the dregs of society.

The second board was to see to the negative aspects of life, that is, the poor, widows, orphans, the aged, who required help. It had to be concerned also with people who had to be put to work and who could be reluctant to go to work, those whose activities required financial aid, and it had to run a kind of bank for the giving or lending of funds to people in need. It also had to take care of public health, diseases, epidemics, and accidents such as fire and floods, and it had to manage a kind of insurance for people to be protected against all such accidents.

The third board was to specialize in commodities and manufacturers' goods. It indicated what was to be produced and how. It also controlled markets and trading, which was a very traditional function of police. The fourth board was to see to the *demesne*, that is, to territory, space, private property, legacies, donations, sales, and also to manorial rights, roads, rivers, public buildings, and so on.

Many features of this text are akin to the political utopias which were so frequent at the time, and even from the sixteenth century. But it is also contemporary with the great theoretical discussions about the reason of state and about the administrative organization of monarchies. It is highly representative of what the epoch considered a well-governed state.

What does this text demonstrate? It demonstrates first that "the police" appear as an administration heading the state together with the judiciary, the army, and the exchequer. But in fact it embraces all those other administrations, and as Turquet says, "It branches out into all of the people's conditions, everything they do or undertake. Its fields comprise justice, finance, and the army."

So, as you see, the police in this utopia include everything, but from a very particular point of view. Men and things are envisioned in this utopia in their relationships. What the police are concerned with is men's coexistence in a territory, their relationships to property, what they produce, what is exchanged in the market, and so on. It also considers how they live, the diseases and accidents which can befall them. In a word, what the

police see to is a live, active, and productive man. Turquet
employs a very remarkable expression. He says, "The police's
true object is man."

Of course, I am a little afraid that you imagine that I have
forged this expression in order to find one of those injurious
aphorisms which are supposed to be my favorite manner, but it's
a real quotation. Don't imagine that I am saying that man is only
a by-product of police. What's important in this idea of man as
the true object of police is a historical change in the relations
between power and individuals. To put it roughly, I would say
that the feudal power consisted in relations between juridical
subjects insofar as they were engaged in juridical relations by
birth, status, or personal engagement, but with this new police
state the government begins to deal with individuals, not only
according to their juridical status but as men, as working, trading,
living beings.

Now let's turn from the dream to the reality and to
administrative practices. We have a compendium written in
France in the beginning of the eighteenth century which gives us
in systematic order the major police regulations of the French
kingdom. It is a kind of manual or systematic encyclopedia for the
use of the civil servants. The author of this manual was N.
Delamare, and he organizes this encyclopedia of police [*Traité de
la police*, 1705] under eleven chapters. The first one is religion; the
second is morals; the third, health; the fourth, supplies; the fifth,
roads, highways, and town buildings; the sixth, public safety; the
seventh, the liberal arts (roughly speaking, the arts and sciences);
the eighth, trade; the ninth, factories; the tenth, manservants and
factory workers; and the eleventh, the poor. That, for Delamare
and those following, was the administrative practice of France.
That was the domain of police, from religion to poor people,
through morals, health, liberal arts, and so on and so on. You'll
find the same classification in most of the treatises or compendiums
concerning the police. As you see, as in Turquet's utopia, apart

from the army and justice, properly speaking, and direct taxes, the police apparently see to everything.

Now what, from this point of view, was the real administrative French practice? What was the logic of intervening in religious rites or in small-scale production techniques, in intellectual life or in the road network? Delamare seems to be a little hesitant trying to answer this question. Sometimes he says, "The police must see to everything pertaining to men's happiness." In other places he says, "The police see to everything regulating society," and he means by "society" social relations "carried on between men." And sometimes, again, he says that the police see to living. This is the definition which I'd like to retain because it is the most original. I think that this definition clarifies the two other definitions, and it is on this definition of police as taking care of living that Delamare insists. He makes the following remarks as to the police's eleven objects. The police deal with religion, not, of course, from the point of view of dogmatic orthodoxy but from the point of view of the moral quality of life. In seeing to health and supplies, the police deal with the preservation of life. Concerning trade, factories, workers, the poor, and public order, the police deal with the conveniences of life. In seeing to the theater, literature, and entertainment, their object is life's pleasure. In short, life is the object of the police. The indispensable, the useful, and the superfluous: Those are the three types of things that we need, or that we can use in our lives. That people survive, that people live, that people do even better than just survive or live: That is exactly what the police have to insure.

This systematization of the French administrative practice seems to me important for several reasons. First, as you see, it attempts to classify needs, which is, of course, an old philosophical tradition, but with the technical project of determining the correlation between the utility scale for individuals and the utility scale for the state. The thesis in Delamare's book is that what is superfluous for individuals can be indispensable for the state, and vice versa. The second important thing is that Delamare makes a political object of human happiness. I know very well that from the beginnings of political philosophy in Western countries everybody knew and said that the happiness of people had to be the permanent goal of governments, but then happiness was conceived as the result or the effect of a really good government. Now happiness is not only a simple effect. Happiness of individuals is a requirement for the survival and development of the state. It is a condition, it is an instrument, and not simply a consequence. People's happiness becomes an element of state strength. And, third, Delamare says that the state has to deal not only with men, or with a lot of men living together, but with society. Society and men as social beings, individuals with all their social relations, are now the true object of the police.

And now, last but not least, "police" became a discipline. It was not only a real administrative practice, it was not only a dream, it was a discipline in the academic meaning of the word. It was taught under the name of *Polizeiwissenschaft* in various universities in Germany, especially in Goettingen. The University of Goettingen has been extremely important for the political history of Europe, since it was at Goettingen that Prussian, Austrian, and Russian civil servants were trained, precisely those who were to carry out Joseph II's or the Great Catherine's reforms. And several Frenchmen, especially in Napoleon's entourage, knew the teaching of this *Polizeiwissenschaft*.

The most important testimony we have about the teaching of police is a kind of manual for the students of *Polizeiwissenschaft*, written by von Justi, with the title, *Elements of Police*. In this book, in this manual for students, the purpose of the police is still defined, as in Delamare, as taking care of individuals living in society. Nevertheless, the way von Justi organizes his book is quite different from Delamare's book. He studies first what he called the "state's landed property," that is, its territory. He considers it under two different aspects: how it is inhabited (town versus country), and then who inhabits these territories (the number of people, their growth, their health, their mortality, immigration, and so on). Then, von Justi analyzes the "goods and chattels," that is, the commodities, manufacture of goods, and their circulation, which involved problems pertaining to cost, credit, and currency. And, finally, the last part of his study is devoted to the conduct of individuals, their morals, their occupational capabilities, their honesty, and how they are able to respect the law.

In my opinion, von Justi's work is a much more advanced demonstration of how the police evolved than Delamare's introduction to his compendium, and there are several reasons for that. The first is that von Justi draws an important distinction between what he calls police (*die Polizei*) and what he calls politics (*die Politik*). *Die Politik* is basically for him the negative task of the state. It consists in the state's fighting against its internal and external enemies, using the law against the internal enemies and the army against the external ones. Von Justi explains that the police (*Polizei*), on the contrary, have a positive task. Their instruments are neither weapons nor laws, defense nor interdiction. The aim of the police is the permanently increasing production of something new, which is supposed to foster the citizens' life and the state's strength. The police govern not by the law but by a specific, a permanent, and a positive intervention in the behavior of individuals. Even if the semantic distinction between *Politik* endorsing negative tasks and *Polizei* insuring positive tasks soon disappeared from political discourse and from the political vocabulary, the problem of a permanent intervention of the state in social processes, even without the form of the law, is, as you know, characteristic of our modern politics and of political problematics. The discussion from the end of the eighteenth century till now about liberalism, *Polizeistaat*, *Rechtsstaat* of law, and so on, originates in this problem of the positive and the negative tasks of the state, in the possibility that the state may have only negative tasks and not positive ones and may have no power of intervention in the behavior of people.

There is another important point in this conception of von Justi that has been very influential with all the political and administrative personnel of the European countries at the end of the eighteenth century and the beginning of the nineteenth. One of the major concepts of von Justi's book is that of population, and I do not think this notion is found in any other treatise on police. I know very well that von Justi didn't invent the notion or the word, but it is worthwhile to note that, under the name of population, Von Justi takes into account what demographers at the same moment were discovering. He sees all the physical or economical elements of the state as constituting an environment on which population depends and which conversely depends on population. Of course, Turquet and utopianists like Turquet also spoke about the rivers, forests, fields, and so on, but essentially as elements capable of producing taxes and incomes. For von Justi, the population and environment are in a perpetual living interrelation, and the state has to manage those living interrelations between those two types of living beings. We can say now that the true object of the police becomes, at the end of the eighteenth century, the population; or, in other words, the state has essentially to take care of men as a population. It wields its power over living beings as living beings, and its politics, therefore, has to be a biopolitics. Since the population is nothing more than what the state takes care of for its own sake, of course, the state is entitled to slaughter it, if necessary. So the reverse of biopolitics is thanatopolitics.

Well, I know very well that these are only proposed sketches and guidemarks. From Botero to von Justi, from the end of the sixteenth century to the end of the eighteenth century, we can at least guess the development of a political rationality linked to a political technology. From the idea that the state has its own nature and its own finality to the idea of man as living individual or man as a part of a population in relation to an environment, we can see the increasing intervention of the state in the life of individuals, the increasing importance of life problems for political power, and the development of possible fields for social and human sciences insofar as they take into account those problems of individual behavior inside the population and the relations between a living population and its environment.

Let me now summarize very briefly what I have been trying to say. First, it is possible to analyze political rationality, as it is possible to analyze any scientific rationality. Of course, this political rationality is linked with other forms of rationality. Its development in large part is dependent upon economical, social, cultural, and technical processes. It is always embodied in institutions and strategies and has its own specificity. Since political rationality is the root of a great number of postulates, evidences of all sorts, institutions and ideas we take for granted, it is both theoretically and practically important to go on with this historical criticism, this historical analysis of our political rationality, which is something different from the discussion about political theories and which is different also from divergences between different political choices. The failure of the major political theories nowadays must lead not to a nonpolitical way of thinking but to an investigation of what has been our political way of thinking during this century.

I should say that in everyday political rationality the failure of political theories is probably due neither to politics nor to theories but to the type of rationality in which they are rooted. The main characteristic of our modern rationality in this perspective is neither the constitution of the state, the coldest of all cold monsters, nor the rise of bourgeois individualism. I won't even say that it is a constant effort to integrate individuals into the political totality. I think that the main characteristic of our political rationality is the fact that this integration of the individuals in a community or in a totality results from a constant correlation between an increasing individualization and the reinforcement of this totality. From this point of view we can understand why the modern political rationality is permitted by the antinomy between law and order.

Law by definition is always referred to a juridical system, and order is referred to an administrative system, to a state's specific order, which was exactly the idea of all those utopians of the beginning of the seventeenth century and was also the idea of those very real administrators of the eighteenth century. I think that the conciliation between law and order, which has been the dream of those men, must remain a dream. It's impossible to reconcile law and order because when you try to do so it is only in the form of an integration of law into the state's order.

My last point will be this: The emergence of social science cannot, as you see, be isolated from the rise of this new political rationality and from this new political technology. Everybody knows that ethnology arose from the process of colonization (which does not mean that it is an imperialistic science). I think in the same way that, if man—if we, as living, speaking, working beings—became an object for several different sciences, the reason has to be sought not in an ideology but in the existence of this political technology which we have formed in our own societies.

AFTERWORD

I want to say how grateful I feel to those who have invited me to this university and who have organized my visit on this campus: President Lattie Coor, Professor Luther Martin, Professor Huck Gutman, Professor Pat Hutton.

When I first met some people in the United States or even in Burlington, Vermont, I was asked, "Why did you choose to come to Burlington?" And, of course, I couldn't answer anything else than, "Well, why not?" But now I feel that I am able to give another answer. I know that I was right to come to this campus. I have a lot of reasons for having enjoyed my stay: The work we have done in the seminar with the faculty, the meetings with several departments, the discussions with students, the hours in the library reading and sometimes chattering, gave me the possibility of meeting with faculty and students in the form which seems to me the most convenient and the most efficient. Through these meetings I have understood that most of us share the same very general views concerning the meaning and the goal of our intellectual work, the usefulness of interdisciplinary research, and the necessity of excavating our own culture in order to open a free space for innovation and creativity.

All that made for a very good time in Burlington. It has been for me a very positive experience. Thank you.

MICHEL FOUCAULT

From Michel Foucault's final lecture at the University of Vermont.

MICHEL FOUCAULT, Professor of the History of Systems of Thought at the Collège de France at the time of his death in June 1984, had lectured at many universities in Europe and the United States. In addition to numerous interviews and articles—*Language, Counter-memory, Practice* (Cornell University Press, 1977) and *Power/Knowledge* (Pantheon Books, 1980)—he also edited a seminar entitled *I, Pierre Rivière, having slaughtered my mother, my sister, and my brother . . . : A Case of Parricide in the Nineteenth Century* (Eng. trans., Pantheon Books, 1975) and published a case study of *Herculine Barbin, Being the Recently Discovered Memoirs of a Nineteenth-Century French Hermaphrodite* (Eng. trans., Pantheon Books, 1980), both of which became the basis for films. Foucault is most remembered for his books *Madness and Civilization* (Eng. trans., 1965); *The Order of Things* (Eng. trans., 1970); *The Archaeology of Knowledge* (Eng. trans., 1972); *The Birth of the Clinic* (Eng. trans., 1973); *Discipline and Punish* (Eng. trans., 1977); and the three volumes of *The History of Sexuality* (Eng. trans., 1978, 1985, 1986), all published by Pantheon.

HUCK GUTMAN, Associate Professor of English at the University of Vermont, teaches American poetry and literary theory. He is the author of *Mankind in Barbary: Individual and Society in the Novels of Norman Mailer* (University Press of New England, 1975), and of articles on American poetry. He is currently completing a history of American literature and is editing a volume of essays providing international perspectives on American literature.

PATRICK H. HUTTON, Professor of History at the University of Vermont, teaches French intellectual history. He is the editor of *An Historical Dictionary of the Third French Republic* (Greenwood

Press, 1986). He is the author of *The Cult of the Revolutionary Tradition* (University of California Press, 1981), and of articles dealing with intellectual history and historiography.

LUTHER H. MARTIN, Professor and Chair of Religion at the University of Vermont, is the author of *Hellenistic Religions: An Introduction* (Oxford University Press, 1987), and of articles dealing with Hellenistic religions and with the theory of religion. He is co-editor of *Essays on Jung and the Study of Religion* (University Press of America, 1985).

RUX S. MARTIN, a free-lance writer and editor, served as secretary to the seminar.

WILLIAM E. PADEN, Associate Professor of Religion at the University of Vermont, is completing a book on the comparative perspective in the study of religion: concepts, structures, variations, and is the author of scholarly articles dealing with the theory of comparative religion.

KENNETH S. ROTHWELL, Professor of English at the University of Vermont, is co-editor and founder of the *Shakespeare on Film Newsletter*, and is the author of *A Mirror for Shakespeare*, a guide to twenty-seven of the plays, and of articles on Shakespearean topics. Chair of the Shakespeare and Film Seminar at the 1981 World Shakespeare Congress in Stratford-upon-Avon, England, he edited the seminar essays for a special issue of *Literature/Film Quarterly*. Currently, he is working on a computerized international filmography and videography of Shakespeare on screen.